Lecture Notes in Computer Science　　　12991

More information about this subseries at https://link.springer.com/bookseries/7410

Kisung Lee · Liang-Jie Zhang (Eds.)

Blockchain – ICBC 2021

4th International Conference
Held as Part of the Services Conference Federation, SCF 2021
Virtual Event, December 10–14, 2021
Proceedings

Springer

Editors
Kisung Lee 🄳
Louisiana State University
Baton Rouge, LA, USA

Liang-Jie Zhang 🄳
Kingdee International Software Group Co.,
Ltd.
Shenzhen, China

ISSN 0302-9743   ISSN 1611-3349 (electronic)
Lecture Notes in Computer Science
ISBN 978-3-030-96526-6   ISBN 978-3-030-96527-3 (eBook)
https://doi.org/10.1007/978-3-030-96527-3

LNCS Sublibrary: SL4 – Security and Cryptology

This Springer imprint is published by the registered company Springer Nature Switzerland AG
The registered company address is: Gewerbestrasse 11, 6330 Cham, Switzerland

Preface

The International Conference on Blockchain (ICBC) aims to provide an international forum for both researchers and industry practitioners to exchange the latest fundamental advances in the state-of-the-art technologies and best practices of blockchain, as well as emerging standards and research topics which would define the future of blockchain.

This volume presents the accepted papers for ICBC 2021, held as a fully virtual conference during December 10–14, 2021. All topics regarding blockchain technologies, platforms, solutions, and business models align with the theme of ICBC. Topics of interest included, but were not limited to, new blockchain architecture, platform constructions, blockchain development, and blockchain services technologies as well as standards and the blockchain services innovation lifecycle, including enterprise modeling, business consulting, solution creation, services orchestration, services optimization, services management, services marketing, and business process integration and management.

We accepted nine papers, comprising eight full papers and one short paper. Each paper was reviewed by at least three independent members of the ICBC 2021 Program Committee. We are pleased to thank the authors whose submissions and participation made this conference possible. We also want to express our thanks to the Program Committee members for their dedication in helping to organize the conference and reviewing the submissions. We owe special thanks to the keynote speakers for their impressive speeches.

December 2021

Kisung Lee
Liang-Jie Zhang

Organization

ICBC 2021 Program Chair

Kisung Lee   Louisiana State University, USA

Services Conference Federation (SCF 2021)

General Chairs

Wu Chou   Essenlix Corporation, USA
Calton Pu (Co-chair)   Georgia Tech, USA
Dimitrios Georgakopoulos   Swinburne University of Technology, Australia

Program Chairs

Liang-Jie Zhang   Kingdee International Software Group Co., Ltd.,
                              China
Ali Arsanjani   Amazon Web Services, USA

CFO

Min Luo   Georgia Tech, USA

Industry Track Chairs

Awel Dico   Etihad Airways, UAE
Rajesh Subramanyan   Amazon Web Services, USA
Siva Kantamneni   Deloitte Consulting, USA

Industry Exhibit and International Affairs Chair

Zhixiong Chen   Mercy College, USA

Operation Committee

Jing Zeng   China Gridcom Co., Ltd., China
Yishuang Ning   Tsinghua University, China
Sheng He   Tsinghua University, China
Han Wang   Tsinghua University, China

Steering Committee

Calton Pu (Co-chair)	Georgia Tech, USA
Liang-Jie Zhang (Co-chair)	Kingdee International Software Group Co., Ltd., China

ICBC 2021 Program Committee

Adel Elmessiry	AlphaFin, USA
Xinxin Fan	IoTeX, USA
Nagarajan Kandasamy	Drexel University, USA
Chao Li	Beijing Jiaotong University, China
Qinghua Lu	CSIRO, Australia
Reza M. Parizi	Kennesaw State University, USA
Catalin Meirosu	Ericsson, Sweden
Roberto Natella	Federico II University of Naples, Italy
Gokhan Sagirlar	IBM Research, Italy
Xiwei Xu	Data61-CSIRO and UNSW, Australia
Jing Zeng	Tsinghua University, China
Rui Zhang	Institute of Information Engineering, Chinese Academy of Sciences, China
Prem Baranwal	Talentica Software (India) Pvt. Ltd., India
Arnab Chatterjee	R3, India
Bo Cheng	Beijing University of Posts and Telecommunications, China
Rudrapatna Shyamasundar	Indian Institute of Technology Bombay, India
Andreas Veneris	University of Toronto, Canada
Jiuyun Xu	China University of Petroleum, China

Conference Sponsor – Services Society

The Services Society (S2) is a non-profit professional organization that has been created to promote worldwide research and technical collaboration in services innovations among academia and industrial professionals. Its members are volunteers from industry and academia with common interests. S2 is registered in the USA as a "501(c) organization", which means that it is an American tax-exempt non-profit organization. S2 collaborates with other professional organizations to sponsor or co-sponsor conferences and to promote an effective services curriculum in colleges and universities. S2 initiates and promotes a "Services University" program worldwide to bridge the gap between industrial needs and university instruction.

The services sector accounted for 79.5% of the GDP of the USA in 2016. Hong Kong has one of the world's most service-oriented economies, with the services sector accounting for more than 90% of GDP. As such, the Services Society has formed 10 Special Interest Groups (SIGs) to support technology and domain specific professional activities:

- Special Interest Group on Web Services (SIG-WS)
- Special Interest Group on Services Computing (SIG-SC)
- Special Interest Group on Services Industry (SIG-SI)
- Special Interest Group on Big Data (SIG-BD)
- Special Interest Group on Cloud Computing (SIG-CLOUD)
- Special Interest Group on Artificial Intelligence (SIG-AI)
- Special Interest Group on Edge Computing (SIG-EC)
- Special Interest Group on Cognitive Computing (SIG-CC)
- Special Interest Group on Blockchain (SIG-BC)
- Special Interest Group on Internet of Things (SIG-IOT)

About the Services Conference Federation (SCF)

As the founding member of the Services Conference Federation (SCF), the First International Conference on Web Services (ICWS) was held in June 2003 in Las Vegas, USA. A sister event, the First International Conference on Web Services - Europe 2003 (ICWS-Europe 2003) was held in Germany in October of the same year. In 2004, ICWS-Europe was changed to the European Conference on Web Services (ECOWS), which was held in Erfurt, Germany. The 19th edition in the conference series, SCF 2021, was held virtually over the Internet during December 10–14, 2021.

In the past 18 years, the ICWS community has expanded from Web engineering innovations to scientific research for the whole services industry. The service delivery platforms have expanded to mobile platforms, the Internet of Things (IoT), cloud computing, and edge computing. The services ecosystem has gradually been enabled, value added, and intelligence embedded through enabling technologies such as big data, artificial intelligence, and cognitive computing. In the coming years, transactions with multiple parties involved will be transformed by blockchain.

Based on the technology trends and best practices in the field, SCF will continue serving as the conference umbrella's code name for all services-related conferences. SCF 2021 defined the future of the New ABCDE (AI, Blockchain, Cloud, big Data, Everything is connected), which enable IOT and support the "5G for Services Era". SCF 2021 featured 10 collocated conferences all centered around the topic of "services", each focusing on exploring different themes (e.g. web-based services, cloud-based services, big data-based services, services innovation lifecycle, AI-driven ubiquitous services, blockchain-driven trust service ecosystems, industry-specific services and applications, and emerging service-oriented technologies). The SCF 2021 members were as follows:

1. The 2021 International Conference on Web Services (ICWS 2021, http://icws.org/), which was the flagship conference for web-based services featuring web services modeling, development, publishing, discovery, composition, testing, adaptation, and delivery, as well as the latest API standards.
2. The 2021 International Conference on Cloud Computing (CLOUD 2021, http://the cloudcomputing.org/), which was the flagship conference for modeling, developing, publishing, monitoring, managing, and delivering XaaS (everything as a service) in the context of various types of cloud environments.
3. The 2021 International Conference on Big Data (BigData 2021, http://bigdataco ngress.org/), which focused on the scientific and engineering innovations of big data.
4. The 2021 International Conference on Services Computing (SCC 2021, http://the scc.org/), which was the flagship conference for the services innovation lifecycle including enterprise modeling, business consulting, solution creation, services orchestration, services optimization, services management, services marketing, and business process integration and management.

5. The 2021 International Conference on AI & Mobile Services (AIMS 2021, http://ai1 000.org/), which addressed the science and technology of artificial intelligence and the development, publication, discovery, orchestration, invocation, testing, delivery, and certification of AI-enabled services and mobile applications.

6. The 2021 World Congress on Services (SERVICES 2021, http://servicescongress. org/), which put its focus on emerging service-oriented technologies and industry-specific services and solutions.

7. The 2021 International Conference on Cognitive Computing (ICCC 2021, http:// thecognitivecomputing.org/), which put its focus on Sensing Intelligence (SI) as a Service (SIaaS), making a system listen, speak, see, smell, taste, understand, interact, and/or walk, in the context of scientific research and engineering solutions.

8. The 2021 International Conference on Internet of Things (ICIOT 2021, http://iciot. org/), which addressed the creation of IoT technologies and the development of IOT services.

9. The 2021 International Conference on Edge Computing (EDGE 2021, http://the edgecomputing.org/), which put its focus on the state of the art and practice of edge computing including, but not limited to, localized resource sharing, connections with the cloud, and 5G devices and applications.

10. The 2021 International Conference on Blockchain (ICBC 2021, http://blockc hain1000.org/), which concentrated on blockchain-based services and enabling technologies.

Some of the highlights of SCF 2021 were as follows:

- Bigger Platform: The 10 collocated conferences (SCF 2021) got sponsorship from the Services Society which is the world-leading not-for-profits organization (501 c(3)) dedicated to serving more than 30,000 services computing researchers and practitioners worldwide. A bigger platform means bigger opportunities for all volunteers, authors, and participants. In addition, Springer provided sponsorship for best paper awards and other professional activities. All 10 conference proceedings of SCF 2021 will be published by Springer and indexed in the ISI Conference Proceedings Citation Index (included in Web of Science), the Engineering Index EI (Compendex and Inspec databases), DBLP, Google Scholar, IO-Port, MathSciNet, Scopus, and ZBlMath.

- Brighter Future: While celebrating the 2021 version of ICWS, SCF 2021 highlighted the Fourth International Conference on Blockchain (ICBC 2021) to build the fundamental infrastructure for enabling secure and trusted services ecosystems. It will also lead our community members to create their own brighter future.

- Better Model: SCF 2021 continued to leverage the invented Conference Blockchain Model (CBM) to innovate the organizing practices for all 10 collocated conferences.

Contents

Short Paper Track

Research Tracks

Agrichain: A Blockchain-Based Food Supply Chain Management System

Vidhi Rambhia[✉], Ruchi Mehta, Riya Shah, Vruddhi Mehta, and Dhiren Patel

Veermata Jijabai Technological Institute, Mumbai, India
{vsrambhia_b17,rnmehta_b17,rnshah_b17,
vgmehta_b17}@ce.vjti.ac.in, director@vjti.ac.in

Abstract. The food supply chain is extremely complex owing to the presence of multiple entities and the perishable nature of goods. In India, the infrastructure facilitating collaboration among stakeholders is very weak which leads to participants working in silos. The food supply chain needs sophisticated ways to gather, integrate and track data published by various stakeholders so as to function effectively and efficiently. Blockchain as a distributed digital ledger technology ensures transparency, traceability, and security, and has shown promise for easing food supply chain management problems. In this paper, we propose Agrichain: a Blockchain-based, low-cost Distributed Ledger Technology solution for the Indian food supply chain ecosystem with detailed design and specifications. The proposed system will enable various stakeholders to register for their specific roles in the supply chain and publish relevant information to the blockchain. This information will then be used to track and trace perishable goods as they move forward in the chain.

Keywords: Blockchain · Supply chain · Distributed Ledger Technology · Traceability · Decentralized systems

1 Introduction

Supply chain management (SCM) is the management of the flow of goods, services and monetary exchanges as well as the data associated with them. This process starts right from the procurement of raw materials and ends with the delivery of the finished product to the end consumer. In general, supply chain activities include procurement of raw materials, product and inventory management and assembly line planning, logistics, and order tracking. Traditional supply chain management systems track and store data pertaining to various SCM activities. However, various entities involved work in isolation and there is no provision to operate on a single consolidated source of information. This limits the transparency and auditability of such systems and introduces a single point of failure even if any one entity is functioning maliciously.

The solution to these problems lies in improving transparency, security, durability, and integrity of supply chain activities. Blockchain and DLT which helps in developing

---

V. Rambhia, R. Mehta, R. Shah and V. Mehta—Equal Contribution.

© Springer Nature Switzerland AG 2022
K. Lee and L.-J. Zhang (Eds.): ICBC 2021, LNCS 12991, pp. 3–15, 2022.
https://doi.org/10.1007/978-3-030-96527-3_1

a decentralized environment with a tamper-proof, secure and transparent ledger can be a potential solution. In blockchain, transactions are recorded in chronological order with the aim of creating permanent and anti-monopoly records. In this paper, we focus particularly on using blockchain for Food Supply Chain (FSC) processes. This innovative technology will ease the management of fruits and vegetables in the agricultural supply chain, thereby enabling farmers to participate without intervention by middlemen. It will also enable various stakeholders including customers to track and trace agricultural goods as they move forward in the chain. A blockchain-based system should record transactions pertaining to the sales and purchases of goods in the supply chain. Smart contracts are self-executing contracts that translate the agreement between a buyer and seller into code format. Such contracts can be used to store the negotiation terms and confirm the results against the agreed terms. The system is decentralized and transparent as no single entity has control over the execution of the transaction anymore, thus providing security by facilitating authenticity, immutability and credibility.

In this paper, we propose Agrichain - a blockchain-based decentralized system for the Indian FSC management. This solution uses ethereum blockchain and smart contracts to streamline SCM activities. To estimate the feasibility of the solution, we have engineered a farm-to-table solution, a prime scenario to represent traceability, i.e. right from the agricultural (farm) side, to the table (consumer). Agrichain provides origin traceability of products and thereby guarantees food safety and quality.

The rest of this paper is organized as follows: Background and related work is detailed in Sect. 2. Section 3 explains our proposed model - Agrichain. In Sect. 4, we discuss its implementation as it stands now along with challenges it addresses. Section 5 concludes the paper with references at the end.

2   Background and Related Work

2.1   Blockchain and Distributed Ledger Technology

Satoshi Nakamato [1] introduces the concept of bitcoin and blockchain in the peer to peer version of electronic cash transactions. The concept of decentralization is described to explain an electronic cash system. The work elaborates on a decentralized consensus protocol in a distributed network environment to establish trust among unknown entities. A number of alternative applications have been conceptualized and implemented on top of this consensus protocol. However, a lack of turing completeness, lack of state, value and blockchain blindness introduces severe limitations on the scope of such decentralized applications.

Vitalik Buterin [2] introduces ethereum and its design rationale throwing light on how it is different from bitcoin. It comes with turing completeness which enables creation of smart contracts and customized decentralized applications. Smart contracts [3] are self-executing contracts. The related code and the agreements they contain exist across a decentralized blockchain network. The contracts are invoked when the system state's meets a set of predefined conditions and then they publish irreversible and tamper-proof transactions on the underlying blockchain. A smart contract can have various use-cases [4] in the fields of Supply Chain, Healthcare, Finance, Insurance, Digital

Rights management and Real Estate where we want to achieve intermediary-free and automated contract execution.

2.2 Supply Chain Management - A Blockchain Use Case

Bushra Mukri [5] highlights the potential of blockchain technology in making supply chain management more secure, resilient and transparent while also discussing the limitations of traditional supply chains like information delay, limited visibility, etc. It concludes by mentioning the various services blockchain is capable of providing in this domain. Fabrizio Dabbene, Paolo Gay, Cristina Tortia [6] analyse how the concept of traceability, technologies and industry requirements impact modern supply chain management processes and discuss different aspects of food supply chain management that are relevant to traceability like food crisis management, bulk product tracking, fraud prevention, anti-counterfeit concerns, quality and identity-preservation concerns.

Treiblmaier, H [7] proposes a framework built on certain economic theories, for middle-range theory and discusses the potential influence of blockchain technology in supply chain management. It highlights the areas and key questions that are to be addressed while integrating blockchain into any SCM and provides an elaborated structure and mapping of the different types of costs associated with blockchain and how they can impact the structural and managerial aspects of any supply chain. However, while this paper provides a theoretical framework to integrate blockchain into the supply chain system, it lacks an application-specific viewpoint of what type of blockchain can be used. It states the scope of blockchain in a very broad sense without taking into account it's idiosyncrasies and functioning. Overall it provides a very generalized approach to the underlying issue.

Blossey, Gregor, Jannick Eisenhardt and G. J. Hahn [8] investigates the applications of Blockchain Technology and Supply Chain Management and develop a framework to create clusters that represent the key features of Blockchain Technology. They map the applications of Blockchain in different industries like Food Products SCM, Container shipping SCM, Pharmaceuticals SCM to the main use case clusters of Visibility, Integrity and Virtualization. While this paper talks about the need for blockchain in the SCM universe, it does not address key issues existing in the current process such as traceability, security and verification. It doesn't provide a deployable solution from an application perspective to this issue as well.

M. P. Caro, M. S. Ali, M. Vecchio and R. Giaffreda [9] state how IoT-based traceability systems in agricultural supply chains often rely on centralized infrastructures, which can cause some important problems, such as: data integrity, tampering. They also propose 'AgriBlockIoT', which is a fully decentralized traceability system for agri-food supply chain management, integrating IoT devices. The known from-farm-to-fork use case is used for assessing the feasibility of the proposed traceability system. A. Shahid, A. Almogren, N. Javaid, F. A. Al-Zahrani, M. Zuair and M. Alam [10] provide a comprehensive framework for SCM in the agricultural industry that ensures transparency, trust and traceability mechanisms. The paper splits the whole supply chain into seven entities namely the Farmer, Distributor, Processor, Retailer, Consumer, Logistic Company and Arbitrator who oversees the entire management. It elaborates on the traceability system, trading and delivery model, and the reputation systems individually, later also tackling the security, vulnerability and robustness issues of the system by presenting security theorems. Andreas Kamilaris, Agusti Fonts, Francesc X. Prenafeta-Boldú [11] discuss the role blockchain plays in food supply chain management systems and its impact, enumerates initiatives and developments in this sector, and elaborates on probable barriers and challenges which prevent its widespread adoption in the domain. Potential benefits of blockchain like traceability, fairer pricing of produce, reduced dependence on intermediaries and transparent financial transactions have been listed.

3 Proposed Model

3.1 Overview

In order to solve the problems with traditional food chain management, we suggest using a blockchain-based solution. To illustrate this, we consider the Hub-and-Spoke model [12]. It is a model that has a centralized warehousing and shipment processing system that resembles the structure of a bicycle wheel. The center of the wheel is the hub or a distribution center and each spoke represents the direction of a delivery. Distribution centers or warehouses are strategically placed within the city from where reaching out to multiple delivery locations within an area (geographically) is possible with the most optimal travel distance and time.

As shown in Fig. 1, the transportation of procured goods in the Hub and Spoke Model has four legs:

Leg 1: The farmer produce is collected by buying centres where the produce is accumulated and arranged to be sold further.
Leg 2: Buying centers transport the produce to Hubs.
Leg 3: The sorted and graded goods are collected from Hubs by retail stores.
Leg 4: Customers buy and pick up vegetables from the retail stores. They can trace their origins using the product tags/ID which is available as a barcode on the product.

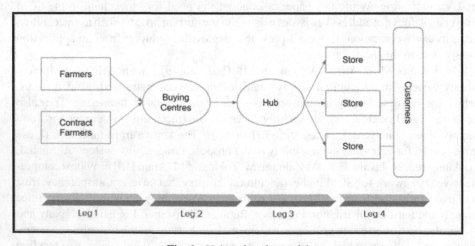

Fig. 1. Hub and spoke model

3.2 Workflow

The goods travel in four phases, namely farmers to organised buying centers, buying centers to hubs, hubs to retail stores and retail outlets to the customer.The various entities along with their functionalities and proposed workflows are:

Farmer. The farmer first registers himself on the blockchain. After registering, he adds the crop information (including raw materials, fertilizer etc.) that he is going to produce on the blockchain. After this process, the farmer sells these crop batches to the buying centres. He adds the transport information like the source, destination, date to the blockchain.

Buying Centre. The buying centre registers on the blockchain. It receives the produce sold by the farmer. These batches are serialized and information pertaining to each batch is added to the blockchain thus connecting the initial information of the farmer related to the crops batch-wise. This helps the buying centre track the farmer's side of the information. Further,the logistics information for the batches sold to the hub is added by this entity.

Hub. The Hub registers itself on the blockchain. It can track the delivery of his serialized batches from the buying centre for delivery. Once the batch is received, the hub grades, sorts and packs the batches as per quality, quantity and price. After this processing, tag numbers are given to the packaged products and this data is uploaded onto the blockchain. The packages are thus connected to the batch number information. After this, the hub arranges for the selling of the packages of the crops to the retail store managers (Fig. 2).

Retail Store. The store manager registers itself onto the system and buys the products from the nearest hub. Transport information for the movement of goods from the hub to the store is added by this entity. With the help of tag numbers, retail stores can track the origin of the produce uptil the farmer. The products are then sold to end-consumers.

Customer. The customers, on purchasing the products from the store, can trace the origin of the product they bought with the help of package ID on the products. The customer will merely scan this ID using a barcode scanner and will be shown the entire history of the purchased product.

3.3 Smart Contracts

In this section, we discuss the implementation of smart contracts. Smart contracts for Agrichain are written in Solidity [13]. They describe the interaction between various entities in the system. The system uses both on and off chain storage. On-chain storage includes the individual entity details along with the various crops produced, and their movement along the chain. Off-chain storage includes the smart contract addresses, user authentication files and application files. Every function in a smart contract is permitted to be executed only by the relevant entity. To implement this programmatically, every

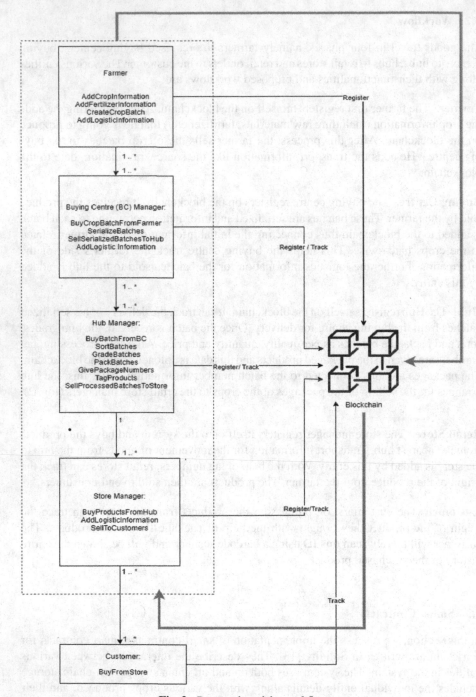

Fig. 2. Proposed model - workflow

function is accompanied by a modifier which serves as a prerequisite check, ensuring that data pertaining to any entity interacts with another only through smart contracts. We have created individual contracts to handle data related to every entity present in the system, barring the customer as he does not invoke any smart contract function. The system comprises individual entity contracts, a Transaction Contract (TC) and a Logistics contract (LC) to handle the movement of goods along the chain and the related transportation information respectively.

Table 1. Data in transaction and logistics smart contract

Transaction	Logistics
string packageId;	string packageId;
uint sellerType;	string vehicleType;
string sellerName;	string vehicleNo;
uint buyerType;	string driverName;
string buyerName;	uint driverContact;
uint cropId;	uint dateDispatched;
string cropName;	
string grade;	
uint price;	
uint quantity;	
uint remainingQuantity;	
string prevId;	
string nextId;	
bool active;	
address sellerAddress;	

Table 2. Smart contract - primary data structures

Mapping	Description
mapping (string => Transaction)	ID => Transaction struct to store each transaction
mapping (address => string)	Txn IDs => Entities involved in the transaction

Table 3. Smart contract - functions for transactions

Function name
Function FarmerToBCTransaction()
Function BCToHubTransaction()
Function HubToRetailerTransaction()
Function RetailerToCustomerTransaction()
Function getTransaction()

To implement and assess performance of these smart contracts in the Blockchain based network, we used Truffle Suite [14], Ganache [15] and Metamask [16]. Truffle enables the user to compile and deploy contracts to Ganache which provides a personal Ethereum blockchain of virtual accounts with pre-defined cryptocurrency, which is deducted as gas in every transaction recorded on the blockchain.We will now discuss how Agrichain uses smart contracts to publish information to the blockchain and use it to track product history.

Registration of All Entities on the System. The preliminary step of the implementation is the registration of all the major stakeholders - Farmers, Buying centres, Hubs and Retailers. Registration details and all entity specific information is added to blockchain via smart contracts designed for this purpose.

Initiating Transactions in the System. The first transaction of the chain is between farmer and buying centre. This transaction includes the cost and quantity of produce which is negotiated and agreed upon by both the entities. Since this is the first transaction in the supply chain, we pass prevId (see Table 1), that is, the previous transaction ID as an empty string (see Fig. 3). In all the transactions from this point onwards, this field will point to the previous transaction of the chain. For example, when a buying centre sells produce to a hub, the prevId field of that transaction will be populated with the ID of its parent transaction (the one in which the buying centre procured the produce from farmer) (Table 2).

```
function farmertoBCTransaction(address seller, address buyer, string memory _packageId, string memory
_sellerName, string memory _buyerName, uint _cropId, string memory _cropName, uint _price, uint _quantity)
public
{
    Transaction memory new_txn = Transaction(_packageId, 0, _sellerName, 1, _buyerName, _cropId, _cropName,
    "", _price, _quantity, _quantity, "", "", true, seller);

    txns[_packageId] = new_txn;
    entityTxns[seller].push(_packageId);
    entityTxns[buyer].push(_packageId);

    emit FarmerToBCTransactionAdded(_sellerName, _buyerName);
}
```

Fig. 3. Smart contract to record the transaction between farmer and buying centre

Further, transaction related logistics information is also added (Fig. 4). Upon the confirmation of the transaction with necessary details, it is published on the blockchain (via smart contracts) and cannot be altered (Table 3). This transaction is reflected in both the farmer's and buying centre's transaction history (Fig. 3).

```
contract LogisticsDetails{
    event LogDataAdded(string packageId);

    mapping (string => Logistics) logs;

    function addLogistic(string memory _packageId, string memory _vehicleType, string memory _vehicleNo, string
    memory _driverName, uint _driverContact, uint _dateDispatched)
    public {

        logs[_packageId].packageId = _packageId;
        logs[_packageId].vehicleType = _vehicleType;
        logs[_packageId].vehicleNo = _vehicleNo;
        logs[_packageId].driverName = _driverName;
        logs[_packageId].driverContact = _driverContact;
        logs[_packageId].dateDispatched = _dateDispatched;

        emit LogDataAdded(_packageId);
    }
```

Fig. 4. Smart contract to add logistics details

The buying centre sells its procured produce to hubs where it is sorted and graded. The hub then initiates a transaction with the concerned retailers and adds required details. The system links this to the previous transaction where the hub had procured the goods it is trying to sell currently. In a similar way, the transaction between retailer and the customer is captured in Agrichain. The packageId attribute in Table 1. is used to extract the details of the corresponding transaction.

Tracing Transaction History. The packageId recorded in the final transaction of the chain, that is, when a retailer sells food items to a customer, is used to track the history of the product. This packageId is used to extract the details of the transaction between retailer and customer. These details include prevId which in turn gives us access to the parent transaction. This process of backtracking is continued till we encounter the very first transaction in the chain (where a farmer sold crops to buying centre).

4 Results and Challenges

4.1 Supply Chain Tracking

Agrichain has a user-friendly Web Interface which various entities in the supply chain can use to publish relevant information on the blockchain. This information is accessible to all intermediaries as well as the end consumer via the tracking feature of the platform. First, a user accesses the UI for this feature and enters a tracking ID. This ID can be either entered manually or can be autofilled using a barcode scanner as shown in Fig. 5. If the ID is valid, the user will be shown the entire history of his purchase along with all the intermediate transaction flows as shown in Fig. 6.

Track your Purchase

Enter the tracking ID to trace
product path

Tracking ID

Track

Fig. 5. User enters tracking ID

4.2 Challenges

The solution presented in this paper, as it stands now, needs to address some key challenges. AgriChain uses the input from the supply chain's stakeholders as its only data source. This makes it necessary for farmers, hub managers, retailers and even the end consumers to have a certain level of computer literacy which enables them to interact with the platform. Stakeholders also need access to internet enabled devices. The process of data entry for the stakeholders might also be time-consuming upto some extent.

Currently, in India, the supply chain management system for agricultural produce is highly unorganized. There is little to no provision for record-keeping at various stages of food supply chain processes. Participating entities will need incentives to migrate from such a traditional way of supply chain management to a blockchain-based digital solution. One incentive that comes with Agrichain is minimization of middlemen involvement. This in turn leads to the elimination of the multiple margins in financial transactions, thus allowing the stakeholders to retain a greater portion of their profits.

Customers who finally buy food items can track their purchase right upto the point of cultivation which makes them trust the system. Blockchain-based Agrichain provides the ability to track the progression of produce, record the information, and show previous records. Documenting a product's journey across the supply chain reveals its true origin and touchpoints, which increases trust and helps eliminate the bias found in today's opaque food supply chains due to centralization, which is eradicated by introduction of smart contracts. A shared, indelible ledger with codified rules could potentially eliminate the possibility of being controlled by any single entity. It also disallows any form of unauthorised change and ensures that authenticity is maintained.

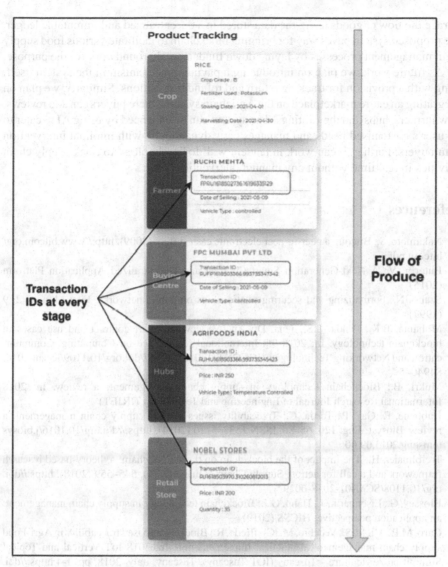

Fig. 6. Tracking product history with Agrichain

5 Conclusion

Using Blockchain technology, the supply chain has gained the potential moving towards complete decentralization in a trustless environment. In this paper, we present an end to end solution for Food Supply Chain Management in the Indian ecosystem which is highly unorganized at the present. The model captures the interaction of various entities ensuring transparency, traceability and record-authenticity at every step. Then, we move forward to discuss how the smart contracts for the supply chain application have been designed and implemented in a functional prototype. The crux of this system is its ability to trace the flow of goods using the data stored in a decentralized and immutable ledger. The proposed system paves way for bringing blockchain to facilitate various food supply chain management processes by laying down fundamental groundwork for the purpose.

As future work, we plan on introducing a payment mechanism in the system itself, along with a provision for tracking return and refund transactions. Similarly, we plan on integrating an entire marketplace on the Agrichain system where buyers can add reviews, view farmers, hubs and their ratings. The system can be enhanced by using AI to cater to the user's customised needs and manages carts dynamically with minimal intervention from buyers. Further, it can work in tandem with IoT technology to track supply chain activities in real-time without any manual intervention.

References

1. Nakamoto, S.: Bitcoin: a peer-to-peer electronic cash system (2009). http://www.bitcoin.org/bitcoin.pdf
2. Buterin, V.: A Next-Generation Smart Contract and Decentralized Application Platform (2015)
3. Szabo, N.: Formalizing and securing relationships on public networks. First Monday **2**, 9 (1997)
4. Mohanta, B.K., Panda, S.S., Jena, D.: An overview of smart contract and use cases in blockchain technology. In: 2018 9th International Conference on Computing, Communication and Networking Technologies (ICCCNT) (2018). https://doi.org/10.1109/icccnt.2018.8494045
5. Mukri, B.: Blockchain technology in supply chain management: a review. In: 2018 International Research Journal of Engineering and Technology (IRJET)
6. Dabbene, F., Gay, P., Tortia, C.: Traceability issues in food supply chain management: a review. Biosyst. Eng. **120**, 65–80, ISSN 1537–5110 (2014). https://doi.org/10.1016/j.biosystemseng.2013.09.006
7. Treiblmaier, H.: The impact of the blockchain on the supply chain: a theory-based research framework and a call for action. Supply Chain Manage. **23**(6), 545–559 (2018). https://doi.org/10.1108/SCM-01-2018-0029
8. Blossey, G., Eisenhardt, J., Hahn, G.J.: Blockchain technology in supply chain management: an application perspective. HICSS (2019)
9. Caro, M.P., Ali, M.S., Vecchio, M., Giaffreda, R.: Blockchain-based traceability in Agri-Food supply chain management: a practical implementation. In: 2018 IoT Vertical and Topical Summit on Agriculture - Tuscany (IOT Tuscany), Tuscany, Italy, 2018, pp. 1-4.https://doi.org/10.1109/IOT-TUSCANY.2018.8373021
10. Shahid, A., Almogren, A., Javaid, N., Al-Zahrani, F.A., Zuair, M., Alam, M.: Blockchain-based agri-food supply chain: a complete solution. IEEE Access **8**, 69230–69243 (2020). https://doi.org/10.1109/ACCESS.2020.2986257
11. Kamilaris, A., Fonts, A., Prenafeta-Boldú, F.X.: The rise of blockchain technology in agriculture and food supply chains. Trends Food Sci. Technol. **91**, 640–652, ISSN 0924–2244 (2019). https://doi.org/10.1016/j.tifs.2019.07.034
12. Agritrade.iift.ac.in. 2021. http://agritrade.iift.ac.in/html/Training/ASEAN%20%E2%80%93%20India%20FTA%20%20Emerging%20Issues%20for%20Trade%20in%20Agriculture/Fruits%20and%20vegetables%20Supply%20Chain%20in%20India.pdf. Accessed 19 Apr 2021
13. Solidity. (n.d.). https://docs.soliditylang.org/en/v0.4.24/. Accessed 20 Apr 2021

14. Truffle Suite. Documentation: Overview. https://www.trufflesuite.com/docs/truffle/ove rview.https://doi.org/10.1007/978-981-15-5833-7_1. Accessed 13 Apr 2021
15. Ganache: Quickstart: Documentation. https://www.trufflesuite.com/docs/ganache/overview. Accessed 13 Apr 2021
16. Metamask. https://metamask.zendesk.com/hc/en-us/sections/360002198491-Getting-sta rted. Accessed 13 Apr 2021

EMRs with Blockchain: A Distributed Democratised Electronic Medical Record Sharing Platform

Parthit Patel[1], Saptarshi Majumder[2($\boxtimes$)], Sanket Shevkar[3],
and Hrithwik Shalu[4]

[1] Cornell University, Ithaca, NY, USA
[2] Indian Institute of Technology, Bombay, India
majumder.saptarshi@iitb.ac.in
[3] Symbiosis Institute of Technology, Pune, India
[4] Indian Institute of Technology, Madras, India

Abstract. Medical data sharing needs to be done with the utmost respect for privacy and security. It contains intimate data of the patient and any access to it must be highly regulated. With the emergence of vertical solutions in healthcare institutions, interoperability across organisations has been hindered. The authors of this paper propose a blockchain based medical-data sharing solution, utilising Hyperledger Fabric to regulate access to medical data, and using the InterPlanetary File System for its storage. We believe that the combination of these two distributed solutions can enable patients to access their medical records across healthcare institutions while ensuring non-repudiation, immutability and providing data-ownership. It would enable healthcare practitioners to access all previous medical records in a single location, empowering them with the data required for the effective diagnosis and treatment of patients. Making it safe and straightforward, it would also enable patients to share medical data with research institutions, leading to the creation of reliable data sets, laying the groundwork required for the creation of personalised medicine.

Keywords: EMR · Blockchain · IPFS storage

1 Introduction

With the rapid developments in the healthcare industry, the amount of electronic data generated by medical institutions has grown tremendously. Medical data despite being highly personal, is not controlled or managed by the patients themselves. Throughout the industry, the authority to manage data lies with the data producer. If a patient wishes to access their own personal data, or share it with another healthcare professional, they require approval from the organisation managing their medical data. Thus, patients in effect, do not own or control their own medical records. Medical data contains sensitive information about an individual. Sharing such data requires a secure platform, demanding high security and privacy along with strict access control restrictions. The lack

© Springer Nature Switzerland AG 2022
K. Lee and L.-J. Zhang (Eds.): ICBC 2021, LNCS 12991, pp. 16–26, 2022.
https://doi.org/10.1007/978-3-030-96527-3_2

of industry wide standards for sharing medical data has given rise to data silos. It has led to vertical development of data management solutions within organisations, stifling interoperability. This also leads to inaccessibility and provider lock-in. Hence, there is a need for a widely accessible solution, which would provide interoperability in a heterogeneous environment and provide the requisite security and privacy that medical records demand.

Blockchain technology is poised as a potent solution for the medical industry. Touted as one of the most substantial technologies of the future, it originated primarily as an undergird to decentralising long standing notions of banking. Besides enabling the rise of cryptocurrencies, blockchain technology has huge implications for data sharing and accountability across industries. All transactions on the blockchain network are written to a cryptographically secure immutable ledger. The ledger, based on a distributed peer-to-peer network, enables the development of solutions requiring high accountability and transparency. Blockchain technology also enables data sovereignty, embedding data ownership as an important characteristic. This allows development of solutions that enable users to manage their data with a desired granularity of access and modification permissions. Modification or access to patient data can be routed through the blockchain network. This would result in a transaction being produced anytime access to patient records are requested. These transactions are written to the immutable ledger in an append only fashion. Ensuring that any change made to the patient data is traceable, it would make medical data resistant to fraud and fabrication. It also allows for the development of horizontal, industry wide solutions. It can act as a secure access point available to healthcare institutions, encapsulating implementation details and promoting interoperability.

The authors of this paper propose a data sharing system for Electronic Health Record (EHR) sharing using the Hyperledger Fabric platform. Hyperledger Fabric is a private permissioned blockchain solution. Users would have to register themselves to an authority in the blockchain network to access it. Hyperledger fabric uses channels to create a private communication medium between two or more entities on the blockchain network, thus ensuring that data shared between participants of the channel is not accessible to other members of the network. The project also incorporates the usage of Interplanetary File System (IPFS) for data storage. IPFS presents itself as a powerful permanent data storage solution accessible across heterogeneous systems. Through a distributed peer-to-peer file storage system, it provides self distribution, removing dependencies on a content distributor. Pairing IPFS with blockchain technology presents a compelling solution to creating an immutable distributed digital solution for heterogeneous systems. The solution aspires to give patients control of their own medical data, making health data accessible across the globe, while the underlying blockchain technology ensures the privacy and integrity of the data stored.

2   Related Work

Relevant work has been done in the field exploring the benefits of blockchain technology in the healthcare domain. Many viable solutions have been presented. In this section, we discuss the relevant work done.

The authors [3] of the paper explore Personal Health Records as a potential means of providing patients fine-grained, personalised and secure access to their medical records. Utilising blockchain and distributed ledger technology, the authors of the paper propose 'Ledger of Me', a PHR solution that puts the patients in charge of their own data.

MediBloc [6], a commercial product uses the Qtum public blockchain. Real data is stored on a Distributed Hash Table on the IPFS, with the meta-data stored on the blockchain. Access control is dictated by smart contracts and has a transaction fee associated.

In the paper, the authors [7] discuss a model for a blockchain based personal medical record sharing model. They expound on an append-only model, the attacks it is vulnerable to and a solution to overcome it.

The Authors [5] discuss a viable solution using the Ethereum blockchain and the IPFS network for verifying the authenticity of online content, specifically online-books. It presents an extensible model that can be used to extend its functionality beyond online-books to other forms of digital content.

3   Background

3.1   Blockchain

Blockchain technology, introduced through the Bitcoin blockchain [4], is a decentralized, distributed ledger of transactions that maintains verified transactions. A transaction on the blockchain, is the primary building block of the system. Using the transactions that are created on the blockchain network, subsequent blocks are generated through a consensus mechanism, after being verified by special nodes on the network called miners. These blocks of transactions that have been approved by the miners, are appended to the blockchain. Transactions are generated whenever there is a transfer of cryptocurrency or input data between participants of the network, or through the execution of a smart contract. Transactions that are pending to be verified are pulled by the miner nodes. They are verified through the consensus mechanism, and a new block is created. This block is added to the main chain in an append only fashion, thus creating an immutable chronologically ordered ledger.

3.2   Consensus Mechanisms

The consensus mechanism of a blockchain determines the protocol for selection of the block to be added to the chain. Hyperledger Fabric [1] does not employ a consensus algorithm, but consensus is achieved through an ordering service.

It can use Raft, Kafka or Solo for the ordering mechanism. Invocation of a chaincode leads to the creation of a proposal. Special nodes called endorsers simulate the proposal by executing the chaincode installed on the blockchain. The endorsers respond with an endorsement response. Once the requisite number of endorsements are received, the transaction is sent to the ordering service, which creates the block and is responsible for the broadcast and delivery of the created blocks to the nodes with the blockchain ledger in the network.

3.3   Hyperledger Fabric

The Hyperledger Fabric platform [1] is a private-permission blockchain solution. It is a platform designed for distributed ledger solutions with a modular architecture. It addresses the issues of confidentiality, flexibility and scalability that other blockchain solutions fail to meet. Unlike other widely-used blockchain solutions, such as Ethereum and Bitcoin which are public and permissionless, the Hyperledger Fabric platform only allows authorized individuals to make transactions on the network. It uses a Membership Service Provider to enrol members to the blockchain network. It is designed to support pluggable implementations of components catering to the requirements of different business solutions.

Distributed Ledger. A decentralised ledger is used to store all the transactions that take place on the blockchain network. This ledger is decentralised in nature as it is replicated across multiple participants of the blockchain network. The information recorded on the ledger is append-only. This ensures the immutability of the blockchain network, while also storing information about data provenance. The ledger in Hyperledger Fabric consists of two components, the world state and the transaction log. All the transactions that have resulted in the current state of the world state, are recorded in the transaction log. The ledger thus, is in effect, a combination of the transaction log and the world state database.

Smart Contracts. Smart Contracts are a key mechanism for ensuring the seamless execution of use-case specific logic in the blockchain network. Hyperledger Fabric smart contracts are called chaincode. When external applications wish to interact with the blockchain, the chaincode for the associated application is invoked. Developers can use Go, JavaScript or Java for the development of chaincode. Execution of the chaincode is initiated through a transaction proposal, and is executed against the ledger's state database at that time instant. Chaincode invocations result in the creation of state transitions.

Channels. An immutable ledger and chaincode is assigned on a per-channel basis. The deployed chaincode can change and manipulate the state of the ledger. The channel dictates the scope of the ledger. If every participant in the network is a part of the channel, then a common shared ledger is available to all the participants. Channels can also be privatised to include only a specific set of participants, thereby allowing the participants to segregate their transactions and ledger.

Peers. Peers are the nodes in the network. They host the ledgers and the chaincode written for the network. There are different types of peers in a hyperledger fabric network, namely:

- Endorser Peers: They simulate and endorse the transaction requested by the client.
- Commiting Peers: Their job is to verify the transactions and create a consensus and add it to the blockchain.
- Client Peers: Using the fabric Software Development Kit, REST servers can be created with which the user applications can be developed to interact with the network.

Orderers. Since hyperledger fabric is permissioned blockchain and follows a deterministic consensus mechanism, rather using probabilistic consensus mechanisms like the one used by Bitcoin [4] or Ethereum [2], the blockchain cannot be forked into different versions which would lead to inconsistency in the ledger. Thus an orderer node is used. The orderer creates a final and corrected block verified by all the peers and distributed to all peer nodes using a messaging service like Kafka or RabbitMQ.

Membership Service Provider. Since hyperledger fabric is a permissioned blockchain, identities are provided to the users. A Public Key Infrastructure is used for creating these identities. A user has a public and private key. The user has to sign transactions with the private key, the MSP on the orderer then verifies it with the users public key. The private key is used to produce a signature on a transaction that only the corresponding public key, that is part of an MSP, can match. Thus, the MSP is the mechanism that allows that identity to be trusted and recognized by the rest of the network without ever revealing the member's private key.

3.4 Interplanetary File System

Blockchain technology is not suitable for storing files of massive sizes. It is an expensive medium for storage of files of medium to large sizes. Electronic medical records such as MRI's generate files of sizes often upwards of 200 Megabytes. This makes using the blockchain for storage of these files infeasible due to its inherently high network latency. The Interplanetary File System (IPFS) is a protocol which provides decentralized and distributed file storage solution that identifies each file content stored using Content Identifiers (CIDs). Every file on the IPFS has a unique CID or SHA-256 hash value associated with it, which makes the sharing of the file straight forward regardless of the size of their underlying content. No information, other than the associated hash value is required to access the file. The file is duplicated across multiple storage nodes depending upon the frequency of access. Due to this duplication, IPFS supports a high level of concurrent access and throughput. The hash size of the files stored on the IPFS is also only a couple of tens of bytes, which makes the storage of the hash values of the associated IPFS files on the blockchain viable. The hash values of the medical files uploaded to the IPFS would be stored in the Fabric Ledger.

4   Proposed Platform

Using Hyperledger Fabric and the IPFS, the authors of this paper propose a decentralised medical data sharing platform. Current healthcare solutions dissolve the patient of the right to control their own digital healthcare identity. Moreover it makes it extremely difficult for the patient to share their medical data because of the heterogeneity in the healthcare solutions adopted by medical institutions.

4.1   Methodology

Users of the system will register with the Certification Authority. Multiple Certification Authorities, managed by the different hospitals would be a part of the Fabric network. The Certification Authority provides X509 certificates to all the participating components in the network. These certificates are required by the components of the system to access the client nodes. Once registered, users of the system would be able to run chaincode which dictates the access control list and the implementation logic. The chaincode is deployed on the peer nodes in the network of all the hospitals. This chaincode prior to deployment has to be approved by all the participating hospitals. On registration, every hospital is given a unique public-private key pair. This cryptographic material are used for encryption of the data generated at the hospital, as well as to digitally sign it. Data that is encrypted with the private key, can only be decrypted with the public key. The private key of the hospital is kept secret. The public key can be shared with other healthcare institutions, using it to decrypt the data shared, thus verifying the provenance of the medical file. A Hyperledger Fabric channel is a private "subnet" of communication between two or more specific network members, for the purpose of conducting private and confidential transactions. A channel is defined by members (organizations), anchor peers per member, the shared ledger, chaincode application(s) and the ordering service node(s). Each transaction on the network is executed on a channel, where each party must be authenticated and authorized to transact on that channel. Each peer that joins a channel, has its own identity given by a membership services provider (MSP), which authenticates each peer to its channel peers and services. In this paper the authors have only implemented a single channel between all the peers, shared ledger, chaincode application and ordering nodes.

The network has one Network Authority, which can be any GDPR and HIPAA compliant authority agreed upon by the majority of the Certification Authorities managed by various hospitals. For instance, National Health Services (NHS) in the UK would be one such authority which acts as the authority

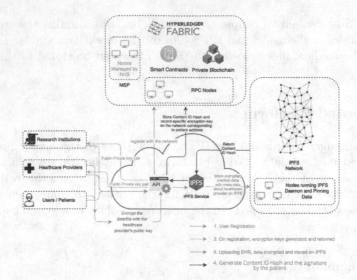

Fig. 1. User registration and uploading patient EHRs

that validates the order of identities for the registered patients. They solely act as facilitators of the network registered patients' identity and bridge the gap between the Hospitals and patients in the network.

4.2   Steps Involved in Transacting Medical Assets

1. A new user receives a PKCS-12 keystore from the Network authority whose X509 certificate is signed by the Network authority.
2. The PKCS-12 keystore would contain a X509 certificate(public key and details about the user) and the private key. This keystore is password protected.
3. Whenever a sender wants to send any kind of data/file across the network, the sender has to encrypt the data/file using the receiver's public key and sign the transaction with the private key.
4. This encrypted file/data is then sent to the receiver along with the public of the sender to verify the signature.
5. The receiver uses their private key to decrypt the data/file and uses the sender's public key to verify the signature.

This same method can be used to **send, receive and store data** on the Hyperledger Fabric Network as well as **send, receive and store files** on the IPFS network.

   To elaborate on the intrinsic process, the hospital/clinic through the patient assigned medical practitioner uploads the patient's files to the IPFS network. They first use the patient's public key to encrypt the file. The CID received after uploading to IPFS is shared with the patient. Whenever patient wants to give access to another healthcare practitioner, the patient first downloads the file from the IPFS network and then decrypts using their private key and then encrypts it using the receiving healthcare practitioner's public key and uploads the file to IPFS and shares the corresponding content hash.

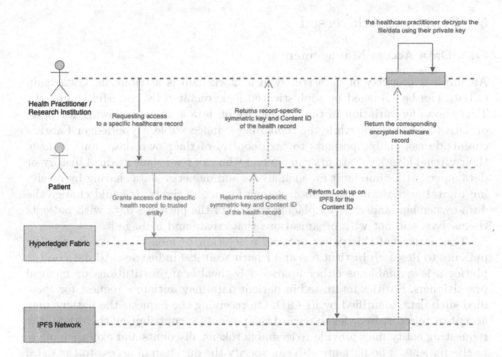

Fig. 2. Sharing a single medical file with healthcare practitioners and research institutions

In the proposed platform, healthcare institutions run a IPFS pinning service. The pinning service handles the storage of the patient data on physical nodes. Healthcare institutions in the system manage nodes that run the IPFS pinning service. The management of the nodes is specific to the healthcare institution, but the data pinned on the nodes is accessible to anyone with the CID of the data stored on it. The patients themselves can pin their data on their personal machines with a IPFS service running, provided they know their data's CID. Patient data would be pinned across multiple nodes. Thus, the patient's data is hosted on multiple locations instead of a single private location. Data stored on the IPFS is addressed by a unique CID generated specific to that data. Any change in the data would lead to a completely different CID being generated. Thus, the CID stored on the blockchain is guaranteed to point to the data that was uploaded by the healthcare institution and patient. Additionally, the CID which points to the medical data even though stored on the blockchain and visible to channel members, is assuredly secure due to the extra layer of asymmetric key encryption of the file during asset transaction. That is even if the assailant can see the CID and access it from the blockchain network, he won't be able to see the contents of the file due to the asymmetric encryption done to the file beforehand.

5   Problems Addressed

5.1   Data Access Management

An implicit property of data stored in a blockchain is attribution. Ownership of data can be managed by sophisticated logic dictated by powerful chaincode. This allows for variation in the granularity of data accessed, allowing for parts of data to be available while the remaining is inaccessible. Hyperledger Fabric's chaincode can enable patients to take control of their own data, and manage their virtual identity. Patients can control who can read their medical history or data, specify the time limit for such access and monetize data sharing by receiving digital or physical assets in exchange for access rights. It could change the data ownership landscape by placing control of the patient's data with patients themselves, and not with organisations that create and manage it.

The authors of this paper propose a solution to monetise data sharing by patients to Research Institutions and Pharmaceutical industries. All data on the platform is verifiable as either uploaded by healthcare institutions or medical practitioners. Entities interested in patient data may initiate a request for specified such data, identified by its CID. On receiving the request, the patient may accept or reject it. In order to reward the patient for contributing their data, the requesting entity may provide redeemable tokens, discounts and exclusive offers to the patients. The patients also can specify the duration of access to the data, dictated by the chaincode logic.

5.2   Data Availability

Due to the immutable nature of blockchains, data stored on the chain is guaranteed to maintain integrity. On-chain medical records or links to the off-chain storage for these records stored on the blockchain are thus safeguarded from tampering. The distributed nature of blockchain also enables high availability. Using the IPFS for storing the medical data ensures a highly robust system. Distributing encrypted data across multiple locations ensures that access to it is not hindered and has no singular point of failure. Encapsulating the patient from the implementation logic, it would also allow the patient to access their medical records in one location, instead of sifting through enterprise specific data storage which is difficult to access and share.

5.3   Data Acquisition

Gathering reliable and ethically sourced healthcare data continues to be a contentious issue for the medical industry. With data ownership belonging to patients, and with access rights managed by them, pharmaceutical companies and research institutions can request access to specific data in exchange for digital or physical assets. Controlling which aspects of their medical records they want to share; patients can maintain a level of control that they previously would not be able to. Not only does this incentives data sharing, but also ensures the integrity of data that the industry has access to. This potential access to large amounts of medical records, the veracity of which is guaranteed by the blockchain, opens doors to many possibilities for the industry. By sharing their medical records, the patients make available to researchers data that is verifiable, authentic and trust-worthy. This data also contains meta-data about the patient which can be used to create rich data sets. With a large enough mass of patients sharing their healthcare data, analysis can be performed on the data and correlation found amongst patients and their health conditions. This can help researchers find patterns amongst patients belonging to similar groups e.g. age, gender and race. Thus, analysing such data of medical records and finding correlations between occurrences of certain conditions, the pharmaceutical industry can create targeted medicine that may cure, halt or prevent diseases more effectively.

5.4   Data Sharing

Although the proposed solution may not be able to solve the issue of standardizing all the data formats used throughout the industry, it provides a common interface through which data can be securely and ethically stored, accessed and utilised. This holds immense value to doctors and patients. Doctors would not have to rely on the patient's diligence to safely store their medical records or tests to access during treatments, instead they would easily locate it on the blockchain. Patients would also save time and money, as they would not have to redundantly perform the same tests. Using IPFS as the storage solution, and the powerful data access controls that Hyperledger Fabric provides, patients can share their data with concerned individuals. This can also be used to further compensate data sharing and lead to provide tangible assets in exchange.

5.5   Improved Research

A reason why many Artificial Intelligence and machine learning based medical innovations haven't been able to find relevance in developing or underdeveloped countries is their inability to generalise. Research conducted and the models that are created, often done so in developed nations. These models use data from these advanced, state-of-the-art machines. Patients in developing or underdeveloped nations are often limited to older equipment that outputs relatively lower quality and resolution data. Thus, the solutions that are created by researchers, often preclude people from impoverished nations. Medical conditions that are prevalent in people from these nations, may not be so in the data sets used to create the solution, thus are not representative of those people. The proposed platform has the potential to create a global system for medical data sharing. This would enable researchers to obtain diverse data sets that resemble the real world. They could procure data from populations peripheral in current medical data sets, and create solutions that would be widely applicable to a broader audience.

5.6 Personalised Medicine

Better research would result due to access to reliable medical data. This opens up the possibility to conduct data analysis of large medical data sets and find patterns within then. As the platform would provide a highly secure medium for data exchange, it can be used for the sharing of genomic data. This data can be shared with pharmaceutical companies for research and development while being compensated for doing so. Thus, it would empower the industry to create personalised medicine, using the reliable data that they would have access to.

6 Conclusion

The authors explored the usage of blockchain technology in the healthcare sector, specifically in the domain of electronic medical record (EHR) sharing. They went over the current problems the current solution space suffers from and how blockchain technology can help alleviate it. They propose a solution using Hyperledger Fabric and the InterPlanetary File System for EHR sharing. They also briefly mention how the platform is poised to help solve some hurdles that EHR sharing currently faces.

References

1. Androulaki, E., et al.: Hyperledger fabric: a distributed operating system for permissioned blockchains. In: Proceedings of the Thirteenth EuroSys Conference, pp. 1–15 (2018)
2. Buterin, V., et al.: Ethereum: a next-generation smart contract and decentralized application platform. **7** (2014). https://github.com/ethereum/wiki/wiki/5BEnglish5D-White-Paper
3. Leeming, G., Cunningham, J., Ainsworth, J.: A ledger of me: personalizing healthcare using blockchain technology. Front. Med. **6**, 171 (2019)
4. Nakamoto, S.: Bitcoin: A peer-to-peer electronic cash system. Technical Report, Manubot (2019)
5. Nizamuddin, N., Hasan, H.R., Salah, K.: IPFS-blockchain-based authenticity of online publications. In: Chen, S., Wang, H., Zhang, L.-J. (eds.) ICBC 2018. LNCS, vol. 10974, pp. 199–212. Springer, Cham (2018). https://doi.org/10.1007/978-3-319-94478-4_14
6. Team, M.: Medibloc whitepaper 2017 (2018)
7. Thwin, T.T., Vasupongayya, S.: Blockchain based secret-data sharing model for personal health record system. In: 2018 5th International Conference on Advanced Informatics: Concept Theory and Applications (ICAICTA), pp. 196–201. IEEE (2018)

Decentralized Authorization in Web Services Using Public Blockchain

Maddipati Varun[1], Muthukur Venkata Akhil Vasishta[1], Balaji Palanisamy[2], and Shamik Sural[1(✉)]

[1] Indian Institute of Technology Kharagpur, Kharagpur, India
{varunmaddipati,akhilvasishtamuthukur}@iitkgp.ac.in,
shamik@cse.iitkgp.ac.in
[2] University of Pittsburgh, Pittsburgh, USA
bpalan@pitt.edu

Abstract. Web services often determine whether to provide access on their resources to a service requesting entity based on the latter's credentials, which may not always be available with a single authority. More commonly, there is a need for getting them verified from multiple external sources in a decentralized manner. This kind of architecture is also more robust against security and privacy attacks as compared to a centralized system. However, it is imperative that authorization by the independent sources be done in a transparent and verifiable manner. In this paper, we propose a method for decentralized authorization using the Ethereum blockchain. We consider the underlying authorization model to be Attribute-based Access Control (ABAC) and hence, the credentials to be verified are the attributes of the users making access requests to the web service. In ABAC, a user is granted or denied access to an object based on her attributes as well as those of the requested object using a set of rules (called the ABAC policy). We use a public blockchain, namely Ethereum, for transparent authorization of attributes by multiple sources to allow the web service to take an access decision. It ensures that the authorization data is immutable and helps in building trust between the users, web service providers and attribute certifying authorities. We have made a prototype implementation of our proposed architecture on the Rinkeby Ethereum test network. Extensive experiments show its scalability in realistic scenarios.

Keywords: Decentralized authorization · Web services · Smart contract · Ethereum · Attribute-based Access Control (ABAC)

1 Introduction

Access control plays an important role in the digital world. In any organization, including web service providers, not everybody has access to every piece of sensitive data. Rather, security rules are kept in place that allow only a select few to be given access to a subset of the data required for carrying out authorized activities. If all such rules and associated artifacts are maintained in a single

© Springer Nature Switzerland AG 2022
K. Lee and L.-J. Zhang (Eds.): ICBC 2021, LNCS 12991, pp. 27–42, 2022.
https://doi.org/10.1007/978-3-030-96527-3_3

central server, it becomes a soft target for the attackers and can lead to compromise of possibly sensitive data. Moreover, in some situations, the nature of the application is such that the credentials required for making an access decision are inherently distributed and bringing them together in a central location is neither feasible nor desirable.

As an example, a public library can subscribe to various journals, e-books and research databases using tax payer's money. In return, valid state or city residents need to be given access to such e-resources. The access control rules in this case would specify which type of residents will have access to which kinds of e-resources. For instance, state resident university students may be given on-line access to journals while local school district students are allowed to access e-text books. It may be noted that it is infeasible for the library to store *a priori* the details of each member of the public at large. Rather it has to get the credentials certified by appropriate authorities at the time of making an access decision. Other pertinent example use cases would include providers of healthcare services where attributes of patients, primary care physicians, specialist doctors, insurance companies, etc., can be authorized on-line by various participating organizations for determining access to patient electronic health records (EHRs). This is especially true in Covid-19 like pandemic situations where physical verification of attributes is not feasible or even advisable.

While several alternatives have been developed over the last few decades, in this work, we consider recently proposed Attribute-based Access Control (ABAC) as the authorization model [1]. The reason for this choice is three-fold. First, it supports fine-grained access control. Second, it allows access to *ad hoc* users without any need for creating their login credentials in order to provide access, and third, ABAC subsumes almost all of the other existing access control models. Hence, the ability to support the ABAC model would establish the capability of supporting any other access control model.

ABAC processes access requests based on the notion of attributes. There are broadly four components in ABAC, namely subject (human user or agent making an access request), object (resource to be accessed like file, e-book, journal paper), environment (conditions under which an access request is being made) and operation (action that the subject attempts to apply on the object). Typical examples of operation include read, write, execute, open file, print. On the other hand, environmental conditions capture various operating conditions like time of access, location of origin of the request captured through the IP address, etc.

The most important characteristic of ABAC is that the subjects (interchangeably called users) are not given access on objects (interchangeably called resources) based on individual identities. Instead, a set of attributes and their possible values are associated with each of these. ABAC verifies the attributes against a set of rules (collectively called a policy) when a request is made by a subject to carry out a certain operation on an object in a particular environmental condition. The rules are also specified in terms of the attributes and not on identities. If there is a rule matching the attributes, access is granted to the subject to perform the desired action on the object; otherwise, it is denied.

In the context of a library service as mentioned above, an access request might come from a university student attempting to download a journal paper subscribed by the library and the request is originated from inside the university VLAN (Virtual LAN). Here subject is the student, object is the particular journal paper, operation is downloading and the environmental condition is the source of the access request identified as the university-specific VLAN.

As is evident from the above discussions, the various credentials (attribute values in ABAC terminology) of the users would typically be available with disparate authorities. It is also only these authorities who can certify the same for the user making the access request to a service provider. In the library use case, for example, the Department of Transportation (DOT) keeps track of the address of an individual from the information captured during issuance of driver's license or state id. On the other hand, the university maintains the details of all on-roll students. Hence, the residency status attribute can be certified by the Department of Transportation (DOT) while the student status can be certified by the university. The service provider (in this example, the library) can get these attributes certified in a decentralized manner by the concerned authorities and then depending on its ABAC security policy, will determine whether to grant access.

With multiple parties thus involved in making the access decision, it is important that the decentralized authorization information is maintained in a manner that cannot be repudiated and also there cannot be any scope for wrongful denial of service. We propose to use a public blockchain, namely Ethereum, for handling authorization in ABAC based web services. A blockchain provides a decentralized means for storing information. It differs from traditional databases by storing the data in the form of blocks that are chained together. This decentralization plays a vital role in ensuring security of data as no single person or group can garner full control over it. Decentralized data stored on the blockchain is also immutable, which means changes made are recorded after verification that cannot be deleted or modified without everybody's knowledge.

To the best of our knowledge, there is no work in the literature that precisely addresses this point, i.e., supporting decentralized certification of ABAC attributes for web services. In the proposed architecture, one or more organizations can assign attribute values for subjects belonging to itself. Over a period of time, these values can also be modified by the same organization. For example, the on-roll status of a student would change after graduation. On the other hand, it is the web service provider organization that serves as the custodian for all the objects under access control and hence, is responsible for assigning attribute values to the objects. The same organization also defines the set of rules or the ABAC policy against which all requested accesses are checked.

Besides proposing an architecture for blockchain based decentralized authorization in ABAC, we have also made a prototype implementation of the same on the Rinkeby test network of Ethereum. Efficient smart contracts were developed using Solidity for executing the various functions. Experiments have been carried out on the deployed system and the results are encouraging.

The rest of the paper is organized as follows. Section 2 reviews existing literature. In Sect. 3, we describe the design aspects of our proposed architecture. Section 4 discusses the implementation details along with an illustrative example. In Sect. 5, we present the results of extensive experimental evaluation of our prototype implementation. Finally, Sect. 6 concludes the paper.

2   Related Work

Unlike other models like Discretionary Access Control (DAC) [17,18] and Role-based Access Control (RBAC) [19–21] which have been around for decades, proliferation of ABAC is yet to attain the same level of spread and maturity. However, there have been some attempts at its efficient implementation. The most straightforward approach from the point of view of ease of deployment is to store the attribute values of subjects, objects and environment along with the ABAC policy in a central database server that can be accessed only by a set of privileged administrative users [3–5]. This method is not sufficiently robust against attacks as it can potentially be compromised by sustained attempts from hackers. Once the attack is successful, the entire data can be stolen or modified in an unauthorized manner. Furthermore, verifying the correctness of the data also becomes difficult as the server logs can as well be overwritten.

Some of the state-of-the-art solutions advocate storing the ABAC system attributes and rules on the cloud. While physically distributed, logically it is not [2]. The cloud might provide a level of security from possible attackers, but its security is inherently limited to a single point of attack and therefore it is vulnerable to sophisticated attacks including insider attacks within the cloud.

Attempts have recently been made to make use of the unique characteristics of blockchains in bolstering existing access control systems. In one such method, the authors use Bitcoin-like blockchain [26] to create an access control scheme for smart home applications [7]. Each home has its own policy list that tells whether an internal or external person has access to the desired device. Even then in each individual home, access control is effectively centralized. While this approach may work well in this context, it is not suitable for large decentralized implementations of ABAC where any form of centralization is undesirable.

In addition to the above-mentioned approaches towards implementation of access control systems, there are also a few schemes where Ethereum smart contracts [6] are used to implement ABAC. A fairly recent work proposes an attribute based access control system using Ethereum where a smart contract is deployed for each subject-object pair to store the attributes, and implement an ABAC policy relating the specific subjects and objects [8]. When a subject needs to access an object, she initiates a transaction to the specific smart contract governing the subject and the object.

There also exist some blockchain based access control systems for extremely custom built applications, which make them difficult for general use [10–12]. In one such implementation, the URL of the policies is stored in the blockchain and a smart contract is used to receive the subject URL before processing the access control request [9]. However, in such an approach, the trustworthiness of the attributes cannot be maintained as these are stored in an external database.

In another alternative access control implementation using Ethereum and smart contracts, the object attributes are completely ignored as it is implemented for only multiple users-single object scenarios [13]. In a related but different context, [14] proves the correctness of smart contracts and deals with various verification methods for blockchain based smart contracts. In contrast to all of the above approaches, the architecture proposed in our work uses the idea of processing access requests and returning the corresponding decision to the user in such a way that the user gets this response instantly. Only after a few access requests have been processed, they are added to the blockchain [15]. A prototype has been implemented that use Solidity for writing smart contracts [16].

3   System Design and Features

The architecture of our proposed system is shown in Fig. 1. The design has several components including the service hosted by the organization maintaining the objects, multiple attribute authorities which verify the attributes of the users as well as the decentralized blockchain infrastructure. In the figure, the blue lines show the flow of adding attributes to objects, pink lines show the flow of adding rules, red lines show the flow of adding attributes to subjects while the dashed lines show the flow of access requests. The numbers given alongside different lines denote the sequential order of flow of transactions.

As seen in Fig. 1, objects and rules are added and modified by the object owner organization administrator using the object smart contract in the Ethereum cloud. At the same time, logs of the object and rule addition or modification are added to the blockchain for verification. Similarly, subjects are added and modified by the user organization administrator using the attribute authority smart contract in Ethereum while logs are added to the blockchain for verification. Next, as subjects send access requests through client applications, access requests are processed by the object smart contract. The object smart contract checks all the rules and determines whether to grant access or not. In the following sub-sections, we describe the complete system architecture by illustrating the four core working principles of this service.

3.1   Initial Deployment of ABAC Components

The web service provider, i.e., the organization that maintains the resources, first needs to identify the attributes and possible values of those attributes for all of its objects. Once this step has been completed, they can deploy their smart contract. This contract has an option to add new objects, remove objects, modify object attribute values, as well as add or modify ABAC policy rules. It also supports addition and modification of attribute authorities, i.e., other organizations who can verify the attributes of users attempting to access the objects hosted by the web service provider.

An attribute certifying authority uses its own smart contract running on the blockchain where it stores the attribute values of all the subjects registered under it. Since our architecture supports the presence of multiple such attribute authorities, each of them has its own smart contract deployed in Ethereum. These contracts are written in Remix using Solidity. Once deployed, anyone can access them using their deployment address. Blockchain also allows these contracts to communicate and share information among themselves. This feature enables implementation of the current structure with multiple attribute authorities that are independent but can communicate with the object organization to authorize the subject. As the actions are performed on the blockchain, an immutable chain of transactions is created which stores the information of every operation.

3.2   Processing Access Requests

A user who wants to initiate any access request, first authenticates herself to the system. She then chooses the set of objects and the actions to be performed on those. Next, she submits the request to the organization owning the objects through an appropriate smart contract. Once the smart contract of the object organization receives the request it first checks if it contains the object that the subject had requested to access. Next, the organization's smart contract proceeds to verify the user attributes. As the different attributes can potentially have different and independent attribute certifying authorities, the object owner organization's smart contract invokes the smart contracts of the appropriate attribute authorities to verify all the attributes of the user.

These verified subject attributes are then concatenated with the attributes of the objects that the user wants to access. Thereafter, the object owner organization's smart contract checks if there is an ABAC rule that grants the desired access to the user. Based on the results of such rule evaluation, the user is notified if her access request is granted or denied. Blockchain plays an important role in this process as once an access request has been made, the request along with its outcome is logged in the blockchain. Since such records are immutable, the organization can always audit all the requests it has processed. Furthermore, the subjects will also know why they were denied access as all the attributes are also verifiable on the blockchain, thus, enhancing transparency in the whole process.

3.3   Auditability and Verifiability

A blockchain is a distributed ledger consisting of a set of blocks chained together and stored in the nodes of the participating entities. Each block contains a cryptographic hash of the previous block and a set of transactions that represent the information to be written in the new block. Computation of the cryptographic hash is an involved process consuming both time as well as resources. If a transaction is altered with malicious intent, all the hash values of the subsequent blocks also will be changed on all the nodes present in the blockchain. This makes it computationally infeasible to alter blocks in the chain making a blockchain tamper-resistant. For decentralized authorization of ABAC attribute

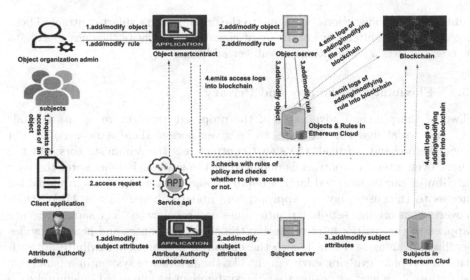

Fig. 1. System architecture

values by independent external entities, it is imperative that we protect the system against intentional denial of service while ensuring non-repudiation.

By writing the attribute value pairs of users into the blockchain, a certifying authority cannot later deny that it had indeed verified the corresponding user. Any potential granting of access arising out of such transactions would be solely the responsibility of the certifier. Also, inadvertent accesses can be easily detected and corrected through appropriate updating of the user attribute values. On the other hand, the service provider cannot deny access to a legitimate user without public knowledge since all the attribute values as well as the rules and the access decision (grant or deny) are written on the blockchain for public scrutiny at any point of time. We provide a functionality for such verification in a user friendly manner. Thus, any denial of service attack can be prevented in our approach. At the same time, if there is any unintentional denial of access happens, the same gets detected and necessary corrective actions can be taken by the service provider organization to update its ABAC rules.

Even though we store the attributes and policies as variables in the smart contracts, we use the *emit* function of Solidity [24] to make sure that every change is indeed logged in Ethereum. This native feature of Ethereum ensures that no access requests, rule and attribute modifications can be done without public knowledge. These logs consist of the event signature (Keccak256 hash of the event name including the data types of its parameters) and the topics (parameters) of the event. We add appropriate code in the smart-contract that logs all the transactions (subject additions, object additions, access requests and rule additions or removals). Once the transactions have been logged, these can be verified by a Python code using the Python library Web3 to iterate though all the logged transactions belonging to the organization's smart-contract. These logs can also be filtered using the event signature to identify the ones specific to access requests, rule additions or subject additions.

3.4 Flexibility, Scalability and Privacy

Two of the principal advantages of the proposed architecture are its flexibility and scalability. For the users to be given access, there is no need to add them beforehand. Instead, the smart contract lets the administrators add the users even after the contract is deployed in the system. Furthermore, the user attributes can be modified later if required, and the set of objects available for access to that user may get appropriately updated based on the ABAC rules covering the original set of attribute values and the new set. The same structure applies to the smart contracts storing the object attributes and hence provides similar advantages. There is also the option of adding new attribute authorities in a rapidly evolving environment like the healthcare system in a pandemic situation. This way we ensure that the system can be expanded indefinitely.

On the other hand, since our architecture does not store the details of all the users from all the organizations desirous of using the service provided by the web services hosting entity, it is highly scalable. The web services host only needs to maintain attribute information of its own resources and the ABAC rules. Similarly, the subscribing organizations keep authentication information of their respective users. Finally, the attribute certifying authorities are concerned only with the particular user attribute they are certifying and not all the other attributes used for access control. It may be noted that most of these pieces of information managed by each of the entities are anyway available with them and are not added as an overhead for supporting the decentralized authorization process facilitated by blockchain in the proposed architecture. Hence, the system is scalable by design.

It may be noted that we store the attributes directly in Ethereum. Since it is a public blockchain and anyone can see its information, the attributes issued by the authorities are visible to everyone in the blockchain. These credentials often contain personal information like driver license, voter id., and hence, can lead to privacy leakage. For ensuring privacy, instead of directly storing attributes, attribute hashes can be stored with an appropriate verification mechanism.

4   Prototype Implementation

We next describe the details of a prototype implementation of our proposed architecture as presented in the previous section.

4.1   Implementation Details

We first coded the smart contracts of the service provider organization and also of the attribute certifying authorities in Solidity, which is a high-level programming language for writing and developing smart contracts on Ethereum. The basic functionality such as the ability of the service provider organization contract to connect with the attribute certifying authority and read the attribute value pairs accurately was next tested in Ganache by running the test cases using Mocha. Once all the test cases were successfully executed, the smart contracts were deployed in the Rinkeby test network [23], which has the complete functionality of the Ethereum main network, using the online Solidity compiler called Remix [22]. Deploying the smart contracts on Rinkeby enabled us to get real time test results such as the average time taken to process an access request.

Next we proceeded to connect to the Rinkeby network for reading the transaction information stored in its blocks. This is necessary for building the capability of transaction verification in case disputes arise, thus achieving non-repudiation and defense against denial of service attacks. To accomplish this, we use Infura [27], a service that allows to connect with the Ethereum blockchain without requiring setting up one's own nodes.

Finally, to verify all the transactions (rule additions, attribute value modifications as well as access request decisions), we use a Python library named Web3 [25]. It facilitates interaction with the blockchain, going through the list of all the blocks stored in the nodes, and filtering out the transactions related to our contracts.

4.2   Illustrative Example

In this sub-section, we take an illustrative example to explain the functioning of the complete system developed by us.

Consider there is a shared library that provides on-line document access services to two universities/institutes. The library maintains a collection of electronic documents (journal papers, e-books, etc.) as files and hence, these serve as the objects in the context of an ABAC model. The library also has a set of rules defining the access control policy for these objects. Let the two institutes be named as *Institute 1* and *Institute 2*, having their own independent set of users serving as subjects in the ABAC system. For the sake of brevity, we consider a limited number of values for each ABAC component as enumerated below.

Each user is assigned three user attributes, namely (i) Unique identifier of a user in her own institute like 1A, 1B, 2A, 2B (ii) Designation like Student, Teacher and (iii) Department like CSE, ECE, ME, EE. Each file is assigned three object attributes, namely (i) File Name, (ii) File Type like Journal Paper, E-book, Conference Paper and (iii) Sensitivity of the file like 1, 2 and 3. Each rule is comprised of four attributes, i.e., Designation, Department, File Type and Sensitivity.

There are two smart contracts used to deploy this system - one for the library service provider and one for the institutes. First, the institutes deploy their own institute smart contract to add users and their attributes. It has two main functions, namely (i) users along with their attributes and (ii) Modify attributes of users. For simplicity, we consider four users each in Institute 1 and Institute 2. For each such user, her attributes are given by the corresponding institute administrator using the institute smart contract. Representative values of the users and their attributes are shown in Table 1.

Table 1. Users of two institutes and their attribute values

S.No	User identifier	Designation	Department
1	1A	Student	ECE
2	1B	Teacher	CSE
3	1C	Student	ME
4	1D	Teacher	EE
5	2A	Student	ECE
6	2B	Teacher	CSE
7	2C	Student	ME
8	2D	Teacher	EE

The library service provider deploys the library smart contract to add files and their attributes along with the set of rules (ABAC policy). The library smart contract has four core functions as enumerated below.
i. Add files along with their attributes
ii. Modify file attributes
iii. Add rules for accessing files
iv. Process incoming access request of users

We consider three files in the library. For each file, the attributes are assigned by the library administrator using the library smart contract. These are shown in Table 2. Notice that the journal paper, i.e., File 1, has been given a higher sensitivity value as compared to the e-book or the conference paper, while the conference paper File 2 has higher sensitivity compared to File 3. The library administrator also lists a set of rules specifying who should be given access to these files and adds them to the ABAC security policy. A policy of six rules is shown in Table 3. These rules are designed as per the current requirements of the library and may be modified as the need changes. The library is now ready to handle access requests originating from the users of both the institutes. A few access requests processed by the library smart contract along with their results are shown in Table 4.

Table 2. Objects and their attribute values

S.No	File name	File type	Sensitivity
1	File 1	Journal Paper	3
2	File 2	Conference Paper	2
3	File 3	E-book	1

Table 3. ABAC security policy with a set of six rules

Rule no.	Designation	Department	Action	File type	Sensitivity
1	Student	ECE	Read	Journal Paper	2
2	Student	ECE	Read	Conference Paper	2
3	Student	ECE	Read	E-Book	2
4	Teacher	CSE	Read	Journal Paper	3
5	Teacher	CSE	Read	Conference Paper	3
6	Teacher	CSE	Read	E-Book	3

Table 4. Results of access requests along with rule number that grants the access

S. No	Access request	Access decision	Rule no.
1	Institute 1, 1A, read, File 2	Granted	2
2	Institute 1, 1A, read, File 1	Denied	NA
3	Institute 1, 1B, read, File 1	Granted	4
4	Institute 1, 1B, read, File 2	Granted	5
5	Institute 2, 2A, read, File 2	Granted	2
6	Institute 2, 2A, read, File 1	Denied	NA
7	Institute 2, 2B, read, File 1	Granted	4
8	Institute 2, 2B, read, File 2	Granted	5

In the first row of the table, the user 1A, who is a student of the ECE department of Institute 1 (Refer to Table 1) is requesting access to read File 2, which is a conference paper with sensitivity 2 (Refer to Table 2). Since, Rule 2 (Refer to Table 3) specifies that all students of ECE department can read any conference paper with sensitivity level 2, the access is granted and the rule responsible is Rule 2. On the other hand, in the second row, when a user 1A from Institute 1 is requesting access to read File 1 with sensitivity 3, there is no rule giving such a permission in Table 3. Hence, the access is denied. The corresponding rule is denoted as Not Applicable (NA) in the table.

Other access requests are also similarly processed by the designated smart contract. Here we considered only a limited number of attributes of users and files, as well as a few rules and two institutes for illustration. In a realistic environment, there will be multiple attributes for users and objects and several institutes can share the library resources using this decentralized system. Since the logs of all the modifications are stored in the Ethereum blockchain as transactions, we can audit the access requests, modification of user and file attributes as well as rules, making the operations secure.

5   Experimental Results

After deploying the prototype implementation of our architecture on the Rinkeby test network of Ethereum, we carried out an extensive set of experiments to evaluate its performance. Specifically, we studied the Gas cost associated with the execution of the contracts and execution time for each type of request that can be invoked in the system. Priced in small fractions (called gwei or naneth) of the Ethereum cryptocurrency ether, gas is used for allocating resources of the Ethereum Virtual Machine (EVM). It enables smart contracts to execute in a secured yet decentralized fashion.

Table 5 shows the gas cost and the time taken to deploy the contracts for the library service provider (Object Owning Organization) and the institute (Attribute Certifying Authority). It may be noted that these are one time costs as they are incurred only during the initial deployment of the smart contracts. Even then, the time taken is of the order of a few seconds. It demonstrates the ease with which the contracts can be deployed.

Tables 6, 7 and 8 show the gas costs associated with the functions of the institute and library smart contracts while Table 9 shows the corresponding execution time. It is observed that adding attributes for the first time for user or file takes more gas compared to changing the attributes later. The elapsed time between a user requesting for access and receiving the result is denoted as the execution time, which is approximately 0.20 s as seen in Table 9. Thus, on an average, 5 access requests per second, i.e., 300 access requests per minute can be processed by the prototype library smart contract. Table 10 shows the verification time for each of the actions performed in the system, It is defined as the time required to go through the blocks and verify the changes done in each action. We iterate from block 0 to the latest block to verify the transactions. This can be further sped up by iterating from the block which contains the transaction of the contracts being created.

Table 5. Gas cost and execution time for initial contract deployment

Contract name	Gas cost (Gas)	Time (Seconds)
Institute	779373	16.14
Library	1694286	15.03

Table 6. Gas cost of transactions made in the Institute smart contract

Function name	Gas cost (Gas)
adduser (1A, Student, ECE)	123777
adduser (1B, Teacher, CSE)	106677
adduser (1C, Teacher, ME)	106689
adduser (1D, Student, EE)	106761
changeuserattributes (1C, Student, ME)	50164
changeuserattributes (1D, Teacher, EE)	52964

Table 7. Gas cost of transactions made in the Library smart contract

Function name	Gas cost (Gas)
addInstitute (Institute 1, contractaddress)	113482
addInstitute (Institute 2, contractaddress)	7928
addfile (File 1, Journal Paper, 3)	139956
addfile (File 2, Conference Paper, 2)	122928
addfile(File 3, E-book, 1)	122820
addrule (Rule 1)	165982
addrule (Rule 2)	148954
addrule (Rule 3)	148846
addrule(Rule 4)	148882
addrule(Rule 5)	148954
addrule(Rule 6)	148846

Table 8. Access request decision and corresponding gas costs

Access request	Access granted/Not	Gas cost (Gas)
Institute 1, 1A, read, File 2	Yes	140069
Institute 1, 1B, read, File 1	Yes	124458
Institute 1, 1A, read, File 1	No	120821
Institute 2, 2A, read, File 2	Yes	140563
Institute 2, 2B, read, File 1	Yes	142052
Institute 2, 2A, read, File 1	No	121315

Table 9. Results on execution time

Task	Time (Seconds)
Add User	11.26
Add Institute	9.61
Add File	15.01
Create Rule	12.87
Check Access (Number of Rules = 5)	0.17
Check Access (Number of Rules = 10)	0.19
Check Access (Number of Rules = 20)	0.20

Table 10. Results on verification time

Task	Time(seconds)
Verify all the Users Added	0.38
Verify all the File Added	0.31
Verify all the Rules added	0.35
Verify all Access Requests	0.32

6   Conclusion and Future Directions

This paper proposed an ABAC based framework for web service provider organizations to maintain objects and get user attribute verification done by several sources in a transparent and immutable manner using a public blockchain, namely, Ethereum. We have implemented a prototype of the system on the Rinkeby test network demonstrating how the executed transactions can be verified if a need arises. Detailed experiments show quite encouraging results.

Our ongoing and future work will be focused along multiple aspects of enhancing the blockchain supported decentralized authorization framework. The first goal is to reduce the total cost of implementing the service by optimizing all the functions through a reduction in the total gas cost. Secondly, in the current architecture, we store the data in the cloud storage allocated to a smart contract and the logs in the blockchain. An alternative possibility to explore is how to store data directly in the blockchain for additional security. A third possibility is to store the data elsewhere (instead of in the Ethereum cloud) and the logs or the hashes of the data in the blockchain. This can help to further reduce the cost as significantly less space would be used in Ethereum.

A privacy enhancement that can be done is that, if the attribute issuing authority and the web service provider are part of a consortium, they can build an access control system restricted to themselves. Rather than being part of a public blockchain, they can join a permissioned blockchain created for themselves. This would improve performance and access handling throughput.

Acknowledgments. The work of Shamik Sural is supported by CISCO University Research Program Fund, Silicon Valley Community Foundation under award number 2020-220329 (3696).

References

1. Hu, V.C., et al.: Guide to Attribute Based Access Control (ABAC) Definition and Considerations. NIST Special Publication **800**, 1–37 (2014)
2. Meshram, A., et al.: ABACaaS: attribute-based access control as a service. In: Ninth ACM Conference on Data and Application Security and Privacy, pp. 153–155 (2019)

3. Liu, Q., et al.: An access control model for resource sharing based on the role-based access control intended for multi-domain manufacturing internet of things. IEEE Access 5(2), 7001–7011 (2017)
4. Yavari, A., et al.: Scalable role-based data disclosure control for the internet of things. In: 37th IEEE International Conference on Distributed Computing Systems, pp. 2226–2233 (2017)
5. Yuan, E., Tong, J.: Attributed based access control (ABAC) for web services. In: IEEE International Conference on Web Services, pp. 561–569 (2005)
6. Buterin, V., et al.: Ethereum white paper: a next generation smart contract and decentralized application platform. Etherum 1–36 (2014). https://ethereum.org/en/whitepaper/
7. Dorri, A., et al.: Blockchain for IoT security and privacy: the case study of a smart home. In: IEEE PerCom Workshops, pp. 618–623 (2017)
8. Zhang, Y., et al.: Smart contract-based access control for the internet of things. IEEE Internet Things J. 6(2), 1594–1605 (2018)
9. Dukkipati, C., Zhang, Y., Cheng, L.C.: Decentralized, blockchain based access control framework for the heterogeneous internet of things. In: 3rd Workshop on Attribute Based Access Control, pp. 61–69 (2018)
10. Markus, I., et al.: DAcc: decentralized ledger based access control for enterprise applications. In: IEEE International Conference on Blockchain and Cryptocurrency (ICBC), pp. 345–351 (2019)
11. Putra, G.D., et al.: Trust management in decentralized IoT access control system. In: IEEE International Conference on Blockchain and Cryptocurrency (ICBC), pp. 1–9 (2020)
12. Di Francesco Maesa, D., et al.: Blockchain based access control services. In: IEEE International Conference on Internet of Things (iThings), pp. 1379–1386 (2018)
13. Hao, G., Meamari, E., Shen, C.C.: Multi-authority attribute-based access control with smart contract. In: International Conference on Blockchain Technology, pp. 6–11 (2019)
14. Almakhour, M., Sliman, L., Samhat, A.E., Mellouk, A.: On the verification of smart contracts: a systematic review. In: Chen, Z., Cui, L., Palanisamy, B., Zhang, L.-J. (eds.) ICBC 2020. LNCS, vol. 12404, pp. 94–107. Springer, Cham (2020). https://doi.org/10.1007/978-3-030-59638-5_7
15. Hwang, G.-H., Chen, P.-H., Lu, C.-H., Chiu, C., Lin, H.-C., Jheng, A.-J.: InfiniteChain: a multi-chain architecture with distributed auditing of sidechains for public blockchains. In: Chen, S., Wang, H., Zhang, L.-J. (eds.) ICBC 2018. LNCS, vol. 10974, pp. 47–60. Springer, Cham (2018). https://doi.org/10.1007/978-3-319-94478-4_4
16. Parizi, R.M., Amritraj, A.D.: Smart contract programming languages on blockchains: an empirical evaluation of usability and security. In: Chen, S., Wang, H., Zhang, L.J. (eds.) Blockchain - ICBC 2018. Lecture Notes in Computer Science, vol. 10974, pp. 75–91. Springer, Cham (2018). https://doi.org/10.1007/978-3-319-94478-4_6
17. Bai, Q., Zheng, Y.: Study on the access control model. In: Cross Strait Quad-Regional Radio Science and Wireless Technology Conference, pp. 830–834 (2011)
18. Solworth, J.A., Sloan, R.H.: A layered design of discretionary access controls with decidable safety properties. In: IEEE Symposium on Security and Privacy, pp. 56–67 (2004)

19. Chatterjee, A., Pitroda, Y., Parmar, M.: Dynamic role-based access control for decentralized applications. In: Chen, Z., Cui, L., Palanisamy, B., Zhang, L.-J. (eds.) ICBC 2020. LNCS, vol. 12404, pp. 185–197. Springer, Cham (2020). https://doi.org/10.1007/978-3-030-59638-5_13
20. Sandhu, R.S., et al.: Role-based access control models. Computer **29**(2), 38–47 (1996)
21. Wonohoesodo, R., Tari, Z.: A role based access control for web services. In: IEEE International Conference on Services Computing, pp. 49–56 (2004)
22. Remix IDE for Ethereum Smart Contract Programming. https://remix.ethereum.org/
23. Rinkeby: Ethereum Test Network. https://www.rinkeby.io/#stats
24. Solidity - Solidity 0.8.0 Documentation. https://docs.soliditylang.org/en/v0.8.0/
25. Web3 - Web3 Documentation. https://web3py.readthedocs.io/en/stable/
26. Bitcoin - Open Source P2P Money. https://bitcoin.org/en/
27. Infura: Ethereum and IPFS API. https://infura.io/

New Gold Mine: Harvesting IoT Data Through DeFi in a Secure Manner

Lei Xu[1], Xinxin Fan[2]([✉]), Lucas Hall[1], and Qi Chai[2]

[1] University of Texas Rio Grande Valley, Brownsville, TX, USA
lucas.hall01@utrgv.edu
[2] IoTeX, Menlo Park, CA, USA
{xinxin,raullen}@iotex.io

Abstract. As a massive amount of Internet of things (IoT) devices are being deployed for data collection, it is desirable to have a marketplace where both IoT device owners and data consumers can trade collected data freely and effectively. While it is possible to build a centralized data trading platform similar to existing commodity markets, it faces several limitations such as lack of neutrality and dependence on external payment system. The development of blockchain technology sheds light on addressing these concerns, and several works have been done on developing blockchain-based IoT data trading systems. Introducing the blockchain into the IoT data market construction also brings new challenges including management and trustworthiness of off-chain information, and supporting rich and fair trading options in a decentralized environment. We propose DTIDM, a decentralized trusted IoT data marketplace, to mitigate these issues and stimulate the trading of IoT data to maximize its potential value. DTIDM utilizes a hardware-software hybrid approach to address the trust issue in data trading and supports various trading mechanisms like selling, direct exchange, and other user-defined trading types. The design of DTIDM is decoupled from the underlying blockchain, so both the framework and key components of DTIDM can be leveraged in an environment selected by the user. We also develop a prototype of the trusted IoT data provider based on the DTIDM design.

Keywords: IoT · Blockchain · Data marketplace · DeFi

1 Introduction

Internet of Things (IoT) devices are being deployed in the field to support a wide range of data-driven applications. Traditionally, one usually deploys the IoT infrastructure by itself and the data collected by the infrastructure will be only used by the device owner. This paradigm has two limitations: (i) The high initial investment sets a high threshold for one to leverage the advancement in IoT and data processing technologies; (ii) It creates many data silos that prevents the full utilization of collected data. To address these issues, the concept of IoT data marketplace was proposed [13], which allows IoT devices owners to sell the data

© Springer Nature Switzerland AG 2022
K. Lee and L.-J. Zhang (Eds.): ICBC 2021, LNCS 12991, pp. 43–58, 2022.
https://doi.org/10.1007/978-3-030-96527-3_4

collected by their devices to others for a profit. Originally, such a marketplace is implemented in a centralized manner like traditional financial markets. While a centralized IoT data marketplace can promote the circulation of IoT data and encourages sharing, the centralized nature does not fit some demands of IoT data trading. For instance, it is hard to guarantee the neutrality of the market and all entities can sell/buy IoT data through the market equally. Another issue is that such a market relies on an external system for financial related operation, which adds more complexity and uncertainty to the IoT data trading.

The emerging blockchain technology offers a new option for building IoT data marketplace and some research has been done along this direction [4,12, 14] by leveraging the salient properties of blockchain such as decentralization, high resilience, data provenance, and etc. However, using a blockchain as the backbone of an IoT data marketplace brings new technical challenges as well. Specifically, a blockchain-based IoT market needs to address the following two major challenges: (i) *Data trustworthiness*. As data is generated by IoT devices that are owned by different participants who want to sell data through the system, there must be a mechanism to guarantee that the data is collected by a real IoT device and not manipulated. (ii) *Fairness of contract execution*. When a data trading contract involves off-chain operations, the platform needs to guarantee the fairness, i.e., the system should avoid the situation that the seller delivers the data without receiving the correct payment and vice versa.

To tackle the aforementioned challenges, we propose a Decentralized Trusted IoT Data Marketplace (DTIDM). Besides designing a secure IoT device architecture that is suitable for trusted IoT data trading, we also propose an end-to-end framework to protect a variety of data trading transactions utilizing both cryptography tools and the special characteristics of blockchain. Furthermore, we develop a prototype of a trusted IoT device that can be used with DTIDM and conduct some preliminary experiments to demonstrate its practicability.

The rest of the paper is organized as follows: In Sect. 2, we provide a high level description of DTIDM as well as our design goals. We present the detailed design of DTIDM and three basic types of IoT data trading methods in Sect. 3. In Sect. 4, the security analysis of DTIDM is provided. We develop a prototype and discuss it in Sect. 5. In Sect. 6, we review related previous work, and we conclude the paper in Sect. 7.

2   Overview of DTIDM

2.1   Participants of DTIDM and Security Assumptions

We summarize the major participants of DTIDM and they way they interact with each other in Fig. 1.

- The decentralized data marketplace (*market*). The data market is built using the blockchain technology to support trading of data collected by IoT devices. Most trading operations are done through smart contracts deployed on the underlying blockchain.

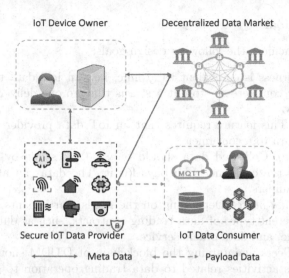

Fig. 1. Participants of DTIDM and their relationships.

- IoT data consumer (*buyer*). An IoT data consumer is an entity who needs to obtain data from one or more IoT devices to support other applications. An IoT data consumer can be either a person or a program. In both cases, a buyer, who is not trusted and may adopt a strategy to maximize its own utility, needs to set up an account in the system.
- IoT data provider (*device*). An IoT data provider is an IoT device deployed in the field for data collection. In DTIDM we require a device to be trusted, i.e., it follows the pre-defined protocol and does not disclose any confidential information.
- IoT device owner (*owner*). Each IoT data provider belongs to an owner who is responsible for deploying the IoT device and collect payments from data consumers. An owner may also facilitate operations related to data trading.
- Hardware vendor. Hardware vendors, which are not included in Fig. 1, manufacture the IoT devices and deliver them to owners, but will not participate in the daily operation of DTIDM.

To support data trading, DTIDM supports the following operations:

- *IoT data provider enrollment.* In this step, an IoT data provider can be securely added to the market and then provide collected data to a potential buyer/consumer.
- *Data contract establishment.* Before an IoT data provider can sell its data to a consumer, the data consumer must achieve an agreement with the provider. A contract in DTIDM is usually in the form of a smart contract deployed on the underlying blockchain.
- *Data contract execution.* After the agreement is achieved, the IoT data provider can share data with the consumer and receive the payment based on the data contract.

2.2 Design Goals

DTIDM should achieve the following design goals:

- *Fairness.* Fairness is equivalent to atomic, i.e., an IoT data trade contract should either complete or stop at a status that no one delivers anything to another party.
- *Correctness.* This feature requires that an IoT data provider is not able to send faked data to a consumer.
- *Confidentiality.* Collected data should only be accessible by the IoT data provider and the consumer who pays for it. The data can also be sold to multiple consumers.
- *Flexible sharing model.* Depending on the needs, participants of the system can have different types of data trading contracts, such as data purchasing, data exchange, and data oracle service.
- *Verifiability.*Peers maintaining the blockchain of DTIDM should be able to verify various activities related to data trading operation to guarantee the system works in a right way and no one can take advantage of others.

3 Detailed Design of DTIDM

3.1 Trusted IoT Data Provider Design

IoT data providers are the sources of the data assets that are traded on DTIDM. If an IoT data provider is malicious, or a malicious owner uses a simulator to pretend to be a real IoT device, they can take advantage of IoT data consumers. Therefore, the first step to achieving the design goals is to guarantee the security of IoT devices and prevent them from sending fake data to the market. Figure 2 shows the diagram of the architecture of the trusted IoT data provider, where ARM Context CPU is used as an example for general purpose computing. Trust-Zone [3] provides an isolation mechanism that allows the creation of a closed and secure environment that is dedicated to data trading related operations. Simple isolation is not enough to guarantee the security of data trading operations. Specifically, the system cannot determine whether a certain program should be loaded into the secure environment and there is a lack of secure storage where sensitive information can be saved. Therefore, the proposed architecture includes a dedicated security sub-system. Besides supporting functions mentioned above, the security sub-system also works as a secure cryptography accelerator to save energy and improve the performance of the IoT device, which supports common cryptography computations such as symmetric/asymmetric encryption, digital signature, and random number generation.

The general purpose computing component with isolation mechanism coupled with the security sub-system together form a trusted execution environment (TEE) for IoT data collection and sharing. Since the TEE is designed for a fixed set of functions, it does not need to support complex remote attestation protocol [6]. The vendor who is trusted is responsible for putting an integrity

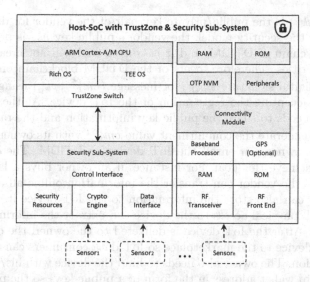

Fig. 2. Architecture diagram of the trusted IoT data provider.

tag of the pre-defined program into the security sub-system and in the booting process the system only needs to guarantee the loaded program is consistent with the pre-loaded integrity tag. The vendor also embeds a public/private key pair into the security sub-system as the root of trust. As the vendor is trusted, we can assume as long as one can recognize the root of trust, the integrity of the system is not compromised. Therefore, a third party who needs to interact with the trusted IoT device can be convinced by a simple digital signature signed by the root private key.

3.2 IoT Data Provider Enrollment

An IoT data provider needs to be connected to blockchain before its owner can do data trading with others through DTIDM. As the production and ownership of an IoT device are separate things, DTIDM uses a two-step enrollment protocol to add an IoT device to the system.

- *Registration.* The vendor who makes the device initializes it and obtains its identity. The device identity is in the form of a public/private key pair (pk_d, sk_d), but the vendor can only access pk_d. The vendor registers the identity (i.e., pk_d) to the market. Note that at this time the vendor does not know who will be the owner, and the binding of the device identity and its owner is done in the second step. Instead of storing pk_d directly to the blockchain for registration, the vendor uses a commitment scheme and the following transaction to register the device:

$$tx_{reg} \leftarrow ((cm_r^{pk_d}, pk_v), sig_{sk_v}^{reg})$$

Here (pk_v, sk_v) is the public/private key pair of the vendor for digital signature. Under the security model, the vendor's public key pk_v is pre-registered to the blockchain of DTIDM, and it is trusted and will not create fake IoT devices identities. Therefore, peers of the DTIDM blockchain only needs to verify the digital signature $sig_{sk_v}^{reg}$ for message $(cm_r^{pk_d}, pk_v)$ using public key pk_v before accepting the registration of the IoT device. At the same time, the vendor needs to share the public key information and the random number used to generate the commitment value $cm_r^{pk_d}$ with its owner in a secure way, so the owner can enroll the IoT device to DTIDM. There are many options to achieve this goal. For instance, if an owner buys a large bulk of IoT devices, the vendor can transfer the information offline all at one time. The vendor can also store the information to the IoT device itself and only the one with physical access to the device can extract the information.

- *Enrollment.* After the IoT device is delivered to the owner, the owner needs to add the device to the marketplace so IoT data consumers can utilize it for data collection. The owner also needs to bind the device with his/her account (a blockchain wallet address in the form of a public key) so the payment can be deposited to the correct account. The owner submits a transaction in the following form to DTIDM:

$$tx_{enrl} \leftarrow (((pk_d, r), pk_o), sig_{sk_o}^{enrl})$$

tx_{enrl} includes both the device information and the owner public key in the same transaction to bind them together. As the public key of the device is also disclosed on the blockchain of DTIDM, all potential data consumers are aware of its existence and can start to buy data from it. After receiving tx_{enrl}, a peer verifies the following information before accepting it to the blockchain: (i) pk_d is not disclosed in all previous enrollment transactions. (ii) There is registration transaction in the system that its commitment value can be opened with (pk_d, r). (iii) $sig_{sk_o}^{enrl}$ is a valid signature of $((pk_d, r), pk_o)$ with public key pk_o. If tx_{enrl} passes all above verification, it is accepted to the blockchain and the enrollment is done.

3.3 Data Trading Contract Construction

In DTIDM we consider three types of data trading contracts, namely data selling, data exchanging, and oracle service.

Data Selling Contract Construction. Selling data, or providing IoT data as a service, is the most common trading contract. For this type of contract, an IoT data provider (device d) sends data to a data consumer (c), and the consumer c pays the device owner (o) of d for the data.

A selling data contract ct_{sell} is a smart contract includes the following essential fields: (i) Identity information. This field includes the identity of d, c, and o. All identities are in the form of public keys. (ii) Data information. This field stores metadata that defines the data that d should be shared with c, which includes the type and the amount of data. (iii) Price information. This field stores the amount of currency the data consumer c should pay for the data. (iv) Data sharing information. This field mainly includes c's data receiving address, protocols for data transmission, and cryptography algorithms for data protection. Both the owner o and the consumer c need to sign ct_{sell} and then it can be accepted by the DTIDM blockchain. After the contract ct_{sell} is accepted by the blockchain, it cannot be executed immediately. The consumer must also make a deposit for the contract, which is equal to the value of the contract. When the deposit transaction is finalized on the blockchain, the contract is ready for execution.

Data Exchanging Contract Construction. Device owners may have different types of IoT devices deployed in different physical locations. Besides sharing their own data for revenue, device owners may need data from other resources, and in this case they can set up a data exchanging contract to exchange data directly.

Two device owners who own different IoT data providers can also exchange data directly without using cryptocurrency as the medium. A data exchanging contract ct_{exch} is a smart contract includes the following essential fields: (i) Identity information. This field includes the two data owners' identities (o_1 and o_2) and their IoT devices identities (d_1 and d_2). (ii) Data information. This field stores information similar to the data information field of *selling data contract*. But here data information from both d_1 and d_2 needs to be kept. (iii) Data sharing information. This field defines data receiving addresses, protocols for data transmission, and cryptography algorithms for data protection from both side of the exchange. After o_1 and o_2 achieve agreement on the contents of ct_{exch}, they use their private keys to sign it and submit to the blockchain. Since they are going to exchange their own data directly, there is no need for deposition.

Oracle Service Contract Construction. Another type of data trading contract is oracle service. As the use of smart contracts extend to a broad range of applications that are outside the blockchain itself, the execution of smart contracts needs trusted external inputs, which are usually referred to as oracle services. Several systems have been proposed to meet this demand [2,9]. Under the framework of DTIDM, an oracle service contract can be treated as a special type of data selling contract. The major difference is that an oracle service contract may work in a passive manner, i.e., the IoT data provider only sends data when there is a request. Therefore, it may take a long time for the contract to be executed. Another difference is that data provided for oracle service usually needs to be stored on the blockchain rather than sharing through an off-chain channel, which in fact simplifies the verification of data delivery as blockchain peers can check the data directly.

3.4   Secure Data Transfer and Verification

Payment processing is straightforward on blockchain, and we describe the details on secure data transfer process here, which depends on the type of the contract. Furthermore, when off-chain data transfer is involved in a data trading contract, DTIDM also needs a mechanism to verify the completeness status.

One-Way Off-Chain Data Transfer and Verification. For a data selling contract, the IoT data provider d uses one-way off-chain data transfer to shares the data with the consumer c. To protect the confidentiality and integrity of shared data, d first selects a random symmetric encryption key k and encrypts it with the consumer's public key pk_c before the data transfer, which is included in the contract. d then uses k to encrypt collected data and sends the ciphertexts of collected data together with the ciphertext of k to c's receiving address. When d has multiple contracts requesting the same types of data, it can aggregate the data sharing to save energy and bandwidth. A straightforward approach to achieve this goal is to use each consumer's public key to encrypt k, but the shared data is only encrypted once and broadcasts to all consumers. After d finishes the data transfer, it submits a transaction to the DTIDM blockchain to notify DTIDM the data has been shared and the system can start to be processed. Peers of the DTIDM blockchain need to be able to verify this transaction, which is by nature verification of the data transfer process. Without loss of generality, we consider the verification in the case of a single data consumer.

Under our security assumption, d is equipped with a TEE and trusted, so it will not send compromised data to c. However, following the principle "trust-but-verify" [10], it is better for blockchain peers to verify that the promised amount of data is delivered. There are different ways to achieve this goal and DTIDM utilizes the idea of network traffic notarization [5,11]. A set of blockchain peers are selected to monitor the network communication between the IoT data provider and the consumer receiving address. Although they cannot inspect the encrypted contents, they can learn whether the correct amount of data is delivered. These peers can then decide whether to endorse the transaction submitted by the IoT data provider to complete the data transfer.

Two-Way Off-Chain Data Exchange. A data exchanging contract needs a two-way off-chain data exchange. While we can use two one-way off-chain data transfers to finish the exchange, this will create a challenge to guarantee the fairness of the contract. Specifically, if one party finishes sending data earlier, the other party may stop sharing. As we discussed earlier, although the devices are trusted and will not send faked data, an attacker can intercept sent data. To address this concern, DTIDM uses a dedicated protocol for two-way off-chain data exchange, which works as follows:

- Device d_1 and d_2 select their own symmetric key k_1 and k_2 respectively.
- d_1 encrypts collected data using k_1 and starts the data transfer process to the address provided by o_2 in the corresponding contract. d_2 does the same thing with its selected key k_2.
- After both d_1 and d_2 finishes the data transfer, device owners o_1 and o_2 enter the next step of exchanging the keys:
  - d_1 runs a (t, n) secret sharing scheme [16] to split k_1 into n pieces, and any t pieces can be used to re-construct the original k_1;
  - d_1 distribute these n key pieces to n random selected peers of the DTIDM blockchain in a secure manner, i.e., only the designated peer can obtain these pieces. d_1 also collects confirmations from these peers that they have obtained the pieces.

- After all the selected peers confirm the reception, d_1 notifies DTIDM that its data is ready to be exchanged through a transaction.
- d_2 follows the same process to prepare its data and k_2. At this stage, both sides have the other's data in the encrypted format.
- DTIDM leverages its blockchain to enforce the fair exchange: all peers who receive a piece of the secret k_1 (k_2) encrypts it with the public key of o_2 (o_1) and forwards it to o_2 (o_1).
- As long as o_1/o_2 can receive at least t pieces of the corresponding secret key, it can recover k_1/k_2 successfully using the reconstruction algorithm of the secret sharing scheme.

– Device owner o_1 (o_2) uses re-constructed k_2 (k_1) to decrypt received data.

The above two-way off-chain data exchange protocol converts the exchange of relatively large amount of data to exchange of small keys. Although each device owner has access to the encrypted data it wants before the encryption keys are exchanged, they cannot use it. The fairness of the exchange protocol is guaranteed by the blockchain. As long as most of the peers of the blockchain are honest, both sides will receive the keys they need correctly at the same time. If any party deviates from the protocol, the blockchain can stop the process and no one will lose its data. We will provide more detailed analysis in Sect. 4.

One-Way On-Chain Data Transfer. One-way on-chain data sharing is used by an oracle service contract, where the data provider sends data to the blockchain as oracle messages. This type of contract usually does not require the data to be encrypted but can be submitted to target blockchain directly. These features greatly reduce the complexity of handling this type of data transfer, and this type of activities can be treated as a special case of one-way off-chain data transfer.

3.5 Data Ownership Management

Unlike physical assets, an important feature of digital assets is that they can be replicated with nearly zero cost. While this is convenient for many cases, it creates a new concern in DTIDM as an IoT data consumer may purchase the data for re-sale. As long as it can sell the data multiple times, the price can be much lower than the original price. In this case, the original IoT data provider has to decrease its price too. This forms a vicious cycle and drives the price of IoT data to zero. In the long run, it discourages investment in the IoT infrastructure and makes IoT device owners reluctant to trade in the market as the return is low.

To keep the ecosystem healthy, DTIDM utilizes the blockchain to support data ownership management. For each data set traded through DTIDM, the device creates a tag of it and includes the tag in the transaction confirming the completeness of the data transfer. Considering the hardware and power constraints of the IoT device, the tag can be a simple hash value of the transferred data set. As the transaction also includes the identity of the IoT device and its owner, the ownership information is established in the blockchain of DTIDM.

As long as all participants follow information stored in the blockchain, DTIDM can protect data ownership and prevent unauthorized data re-sale. If one wants to sell the same data set it bought from another party, the blockchain peers treat the activity as a type of *double spending* and the corresponding transaction will be rejected. One way to enforce the instructions managed by the DTIDM blockchain is to require all participants who consume IoT data to be equipped with a TEE (e.g., Intel SGX [1] and AMD SEV [15] for desktop/server TEE), not only the IoT data providers. The TEE creates an enclave that is configured to work with DTIDM. When an IoT data provider sends data to a consumer, the data encryption key is shared with the enclave, not the owner of the data consumer. Therefore, the transferred data can only be decrypted inside the enclave and cannot be exported to the outside environment for resale. At the same time, the enclave also checks the ownership information of any input data on the blockchain, and only accepts the input data if it is authorized to consume it. The effectiveness of this ownership management method heavily depends on the acceptance of the DTIDM. When more participants sell their IoT data through DTIDM, DTIDM can attract more IoT data consumers and be in a favorable position in enforcing the adoption of TEE.

3.6   Reducing IoT Device Interaction with Blockchain

In DTIDM, most of the blockchain transaction verification can be done by the device owners, who can operate more powerful machines to interact with DTIDM or participate in the DTIDM blockchain maintenance. Although a device owner is not trusted, it is rational and will be honest when it is the best strategy for its own interest. To enable delegated transaction verification, the owner only needs to embed its public key into the device when deploying it to the field. The TEE of the device can prevent an adversary from compromising this information. If the owner believes a transaction has been confirmed on the blockchain, it can notify the IoT device with the original blockchain transaction with its digital signature. The owner can verify several types of transactions on behalf of its IoT devices: (i) Validity of a contract. A contract defines the data trading operations a device needs to follow, and the device must be convinced it follows the correct instructions. The owner does not have an incentive to cheat on a contract. If it is not satisfied with the contract, it does not need to enter the trading from the beginning. (ii) Validity of deposit. A deposit is related to a data selling contract and made by an IoT data consumer. The device owner will not ignore a deposit transaction or cheat the IoT device with a fake transaction (e.g., using replay attack), as the goal of the deposit is to make sure the IoT device owner can receive payment after the data is successfully delivered.

3.7   Management and Maintenance of Underlying Blockchain

DTIDM relies on the underlying blockchain for various operations, especially those related to data trading contracts processing and payment settlement. The design of DTIDM intends to avoid being coupled with any specific blockchain system, and the protocols described above can be implemented on top of almost any blockchain platform. Considering the nature of IoT data trading, it is better for the blockchain system to satisfy several requirements:

- Global order. While the local order (i.e., there is an absolute order for transactions related to the same trading) is enough to guarantee the correctness of simple data trading/exchange contract, it is not enough to handle situations where multiple data trading are interdependent.
- Quick finalization. When an IoT data consumer relies on purchased data for time sensitive applications, the latency becomes crucial. Therefore, it is better for the selected blockchain to finalize transactions quickly.
- High throughput. As more IoT data is traded on DTIDM and more derivative tools are developed, the number of transactions submitted to the blockchain can explode.
- Decentralization. To better facilitate IoT data trading, it is better to maintain a dedicated cryptocurrency system on the same blockchain. To avoid the payment system being manipulated by a small number of peers, the blockchain needs to be resilient against centralization. This also guarantees the neutrality of DTIDM.

Another factor that needs to be considered is the support of two-way off-chain data exchange. For this operation, blockchain peers are utilized for fair secret key exchange, and some peers are selected to temporarily hold secret key splits. If a permissioned blockchain is used, DTIDM only needs to randomize the selection process among all available peers for secret key splits. When a public blockchain is used, the selection process is more complex and potential attacks such as Sybil attacks [8], i.e., many selected peers are controlled by the same attacker and the attacker can recover the secret key used for data encryption. Many works have been done on protecting a public blockchain from such attacks [17] and can be utilized by DTIDM.

4   Analysis of DTIDM

In this section, we analyze the security features of DTIDM and demonstrate that it meets the design goals given in Sect. 2.

Fairness. Fairness is mainly achieved through the blockchain. For the basic data selling process, the blockchain safely holds the buyer's deposit and verifies the completeness of data transfer. Unless one participant terminates the contract before the start of data delivery, the blockchain will enforce the payment after the consumer receives purchased data. For direct data exchange, as long as the attacker cannot compromise the (t, n) secret sharing scheme (less than t peers are controlled by the attacker) and there are enough honest peers (more than t peers are honest and follow the protocol).

Correctness. The correctness feature is mainly achieved through the TEE of IoT data providers. The sensors for data collection is connected to the secure execution environment provided by the TEE directly, and the data sending function and contract parsing/execution function are also protected by the TEE. Therefore, an attacker cannot tamper with the data delivery process as long as the TEE is secure. Although an IoT device sometimes relies on its owner to confirm whether a transaction is included in the blockchain as discussed in Sect. 3.6, this will not affect the correctness of transferred data. The only attack an IoT device owner can do is denial-of-service, i.e., after achieving agreement with the data consumer, the owner does not notify the IoT device to send data. In this case, the consumer can find another source for the data and DTIDM can define a policy to remove such participants from the market.

Confidentiality. All traded data is encrypted before sending through the network, so the data confidentiality is reduced to the safety of keys. The secret key is selected by an IoT data provider using TEE so the attacker cannot access it. The secret key is then sealed with consumer's public key and only the one with corresponding private key can recover the secret key. Therefore, the secret key is safe if the IoT data consumer keeps its private key safe.

For the two-way off-chain data exchange, a (t, n) secret sharing scheme is used to support fair data exchange. If an attacker manages to compromise more than t peers that are selected to hold a secret key splits, it can break the confidentiality. The two parameters t and n are determined by the IoT data provider and consumer together. If there is a higher level of requirement on confidentiality, larger t and n can be selected to reduce the success probability of the attacker.

Flexible Sharing Model. DTIDM is able to support a variety of data trading contracts, including, but not limited to, data selling, data exchanging, and oracle service. Participants can create new types of contracts to support other novel data trading tools.

Verifiability. All data trading operations are done with a sequence of blockchain transactions, which are verified by peers of the blockchain before accepted. These transactions include the agreed trading contract, deposit, data transfer statuses, and payment statuses. For all the critical steps, the blockchain peers verify the information correctness and evidence is preserved on the blockchain.

5 Prototypes and Implementation

5.1 Prototype of Trusted IoT Data Provider

We implement a prototype of the trusted IoT data provider as showed in Fig. 3. The prototype is based on NORDIC nRF9160 [7], a compact and fully-integrated System-in-Package (SiP). It uses a 64 MHz ARM Cortex-M33 processor with 1 MB of on-chip flash and 256 KB of RAM, which makes advanced cellular-IoT applications possible with a single-device solution. An integrated cellular-IoT modem for LTE-M & NB-IoT allows the prototype to operate globally and to connect with mobile network operators via SIM card.

Fig. 3. The prototype of trusted IoT data provider.

From security perspective, the prototype uses ARM TrustZone to isolate security sensitive operations such as parsing of contracts and data collection into the secure world, and the ARM CryptoCell 310 is utilized as the security sub-system as demonstrated in Fig. 2. We conduct preliminary experiments on the major cryptography operations and summarize the results in Table 1.

Table 1. Cryptography operation performance with CryptoCell 310

Operation	Parameters	Time
AES ECB encryption	128-bit key, 512-byte input	523.5 μs
AES ECB decryption	128-bit key, 512-byte input	514.2 μs
SHA256	512-byte input	784.3 μs
ECDSA sign (secp256r1)	32 bytes input	34.87 ms
ECDSA verify (secp256r1)	32 bytes input	37.46 ms

5.2   Number of Transactions for Data Trading

As we discussed in Sect. 3, DTIDM can work with different blockchain platforms. Since there is no one-size-fits-all blockchain platform, the trading platform designer needs to weigh the pros and cons of different options to select one fits the demand. It does not matter what blockchain platform is used to build DTIDM, the number of transactions needed to finish a trade is always an important metric, especially for the throughput of the system. Table 2 summarizes the number of transactions involved for major types of IoT data trading on DTIDM.

Table 2. Number of blockchain transactions for one IoT data trade.

Type of data trading	Number of TXs
Data selling	4: 1 (tx of contract) + 1 (tx of deposit) + 1 (tx of data transfer) + 1 (tx of payment)
Data exchange	7: 1 (tx of contract) + 2 (tx of data transfer) + 2 (tx of key distribution) + 1 (tx of exchange confirmation)
Selling/buying of contract of contract	2: 1 (tx of new contract) + 1 (tx of payment)

6   Related Works

Özyilmaz *et al.* presented a blockchain based IoT data market in [14]. It discussed implementation using both private and public blockchain platforms including Corda and IOTA, but largely ignored other aspects of an IoT data market, such as rich trading options and related fairness/confidentiality/correctness issues. Badreddine *et al.* proposed to use a pub/sub model for data trading and focused on the traceability issue in [4]. Compared with DTIDM, this work considered limited types of trading. Furthermore, the proposed tracing schemes can also be integrated into DTIDM to offer a trade-off between cost and traceability. Li *et al.* developed an IoT data sharing system BDDT [12]. BDDT did not consider fairness issue and only considered a single type of data trading, i.e., an IoT data provider selling data to a consumer. We summarize the comparison results in Table 3.

Table 3. Comparison with other blockchain based IoT market systems.

	Fairness	Correctness	Confidentiality	Flexible sharing	Verifiability
[14]	✓	not discussed	✓	✗	✓
[4]	✓	not discussed	not discussed	✗	✓
[12]	✗	not discussed	✓	✗	✓
DTIDM	✓	✓	✓	✓	✓

7   Conclusion

Data has become an important resource for modern economy, and the massive amount of IoT devices has become one of the most important data sources. As an emerging decentralization platform, blockchain offers many desirable features and is a promising technology for the construction of an IoT data market. The proposed DTIDM addresses several of the most important technique challenges for such a market system, including design of trusted IoT data provider, participant management, fairness/richness of trading operations, and other security concerns. Although DTIDM relies on the underlying blockchain for many operations, most of its components will work with a generic blockchain system, which gives the user the freedom to choose the most appropriate one based on the demands of the trading system.

References

1. Intel Software Guard Extensions Programming Reference, October 2014. https://software.intel.com/sites/default/files/managed/48/88/329298-002.pdf
2. Adler, J., Berryhill, R., Veneris, A., Poulos, Z., Veira, N., Kastania, A.: Astraea: a decentralized blockchain oracle. In: 2018 IEEE international conference on internet of things (IThings) and IEEE green computing and communications (GreenCom) and IEEE cyber, physical and social computing (CPSCom) and IEEE smart data (SmartData), pp. 1145–1152. IEEE (2018)
3. ARM: Arm security technology building a secure system using trustzone technology (2009)
4. Badreddine, W., Zhang, K., Talhi, C.: Monetization using blockchains for IoT data marketplace. In: 2020 IEEE International Conference on Blockchain and Cryptocurrency (ICBC), pp. 1–9. IEEE (2020)
5. Chowdhury, M.J.M., Colman, A., Kabir, M.A., Han, J., Sarda, P.: Blockchain as a notarization service for data sharing with personal data store. In: 2018 17th IEEE International Conference on Trust, Security and Privacy in Computing and Communications/12th IEEE International Conference on Big Data Science and Engineering (TrustCom/BigDataSE), pp. 1330–1335. IEEE (2018)
6. Coker, G., Guttman, J., Loscocco, P., Herzog, A., Millen, J., O'Hanlon, B., Ramsdell, J., Segall, A., Sheehy, J., Sniffen, B.: Principles of remote attestation. Int. J. Inf. Secur. **10**(2), 63–81 (2011)
7. Damslora, B.J.: Data collection in a cellular sensor network with nRF9160. Master's thesis, NTNU (2019)
8. Douceur, J.R.: The sybil attack. In: International Workshop on Peer-to-Peer Systems, pp. 251–260. Springer (2002)
9. Ellis, S., Juels, A., Nazarov, S.: Chainlink: a decentralized oracle network (2017). https://link.smartcontract.com/whitepaper
10. Gundlach, G.T., Cannon, J.P.: "trust but verify"? the performance implications of verification strategies in trusting relationships. J. Acad. Mark. Sci. **38**(4), 399–417 (2010)
11. Kleinaki, A.S., Mytis-Gkometh, P., Drosatos, G., Efraimidis, P.S., Kaldoudi, E.: A blockchain-based notarization service for biomedical knowledge retrieval. Comput. Struct. Biotechnol. J. **16**, 288–297 (2018)
12. Li, H., Pei, L., Liao, D., Wang, X., Xu, D., Sun, J.: BDDT: use blockchain to facilitate iot data transactions. Cluster Computing, pp. 1–15 (2020)
13. Mišura, K., Žagar, M.: Data marketplace for internet of things. In: 2016 International Conference on Smart Systems and Technologies (SST), pp. 255–260. IEEE (2016)

14. Özyilmaz, K.R., Doğan, M., Yurdakul, A.: IDMoB: IoT data marketplace on blockchain. In: 2018 Crypto Valley Conference on Blockchain Technology (CVCBT), pp. 11–19. IEEE (2018)
15. SEV-SNP, A.: Strengthening vm isolation with integrity protection and more. White Paper, January 2020
16. Shamir, A.: How to share a secret. Commun. ACM **22**(11), 612–613 (1979)
17. Swathi, P., Modi, C., Patel, D.: Preventing sybil attack in blockchain using distributed behavior monitoring of miners. In: 2019 10th International Conference on Computing, Communication and Networking Technologies (ICCCNT), pp. 1–6. IEEE (2019)

Alternative Difficulty Adjustment Algorithms for Preventing Selfish Mining Attack

Hamid Azimy$^{(\boxtimes)}$ and Ali Ghorbani

University of New Brunswick, Fredericton, Canada
{hazimy,ghorbani}@unb.ca

Abstract. Selfish mining is one of the most famous attacks on the mining process of Bitcoin and other Proof-of-Work blockchains in general. So, preventing selfish mining is an important objective. There have been a few attempts to prevent selfish mining. In this work, we focus on alternative difficulty adjustment algorithms that try to discourage selfish miners by extending their waiting time for selfish mining to become profitable, Zeno's DAA in particular. We propose two extensions on Zeno's DAA: 1) Zeno's Max DAA, which increase the difficulty in one step but decreases it in multiple steps, and 2) Zeno's Parametric DAA that has a parameter that can be tuned to control the rate of the decrement (or increment) in the value of difficulty. We evaluate these two alternatives DAAs and show that Zeno's Max performs better than Zeno's for scalability of the network and scales the network faster. Also, Zeno's Parametric is a family of DAAs that not only has the default DAA and Zeno's DAA as its members but also can include anything in between or even DAAs more conservative than Zeno's, which decrease the difficulty even slower than Zeno's.

Keywords: Bitcoin network · Blockchain · Selfish mining · Difficulty adjustment algorithm

1 Introduction

Bitcoin network aims to keep the *block generation rate* constant, so the whole network generates a block every ten minutes on average. By the network growing, the difficulty also needs to increase proportionally and vice versa. In Bitcoin's protocol, this happens almost every two weeks, or more specifically, every 2016 block. This process is known as the *difficulty adjustment* process.

Bitcoin's default Difficulty Adjustment Algorithm (DAA) is very simple: at the end of a period of 2016 blocks, all the nodes in the Bitcoin network calculate the ratio of *expected block generation rate* to the *actual block generation rate*. This ratio shows the actual difficulty value for the previous period, which is then multiplied by the current difficulty value to produce the next difficulty value. By

© Springer Nature Switzerland AG 2022
K. Lee and L.-J. Zhang (Eds.): ICBC 2021, LNCS 12991, pp. 59–73, 2022.
https://doi.org/10.1007/978-3-030-96527-3_5

doing so, the *difficulty value* of the next period is set proportional to the actual *difficulty value* of the previous period.

Given the simplicity of the difficulty adjustment algorithm, some malicious Bitcoin miners have exhibited behaviour that is often known as *selfish mining*, first introduced by Eyal and Sirer [9]. Selfish mining attempts to maximize the profitability of the attacker through strategies such as hiding generated blocks from the main blockchain. There has been some conflicting evidence on how effective selfish mining attacks could be. We talk about selfish mining in more detail in the following sections.

There have been a few attempts to prevent selfish mining. One of them is Zeno's DAA [2] that pays attention to the vulnerability of Bitcoin's default DAA. Our goal in this paper is to extend this algorithm and fix its shortcomings.

The rest of the paper is organized as follows. In Sect. 2 we will go through the related works, review threats and attacks to the Bitcoin network and blockchain, and discuss some countermeasures. Our proposed methods will be introduced in Sect. 3. In Sect. 4, we will evaluate our proposed method and present the results. Finally, in Sect. 5 we will conclude our work and discuss potential future works.

2   Literature Review

In recent years, blockchain has received growing attention [4] in domains such as financial services, insurance, healthcare, voting systems, IoT, and smart city, cloud storage, to name a few. This naturally leads to a variety of threats towards the blockchain structure and its mining process [25]. In a broader view, we can categorize Bitcoin threats into two major categories: *privacy issues* and *security issues*. Conti et al. have surveyed these issues in their paper [6]. In this paper, we mainly focus on security issues in the bitcoin mining process, and more specifically, selfish mining.

2.1   Security of Bitcoin

Our focus in this paper is on attacks against the mining process or, in other words, the peer-to-peer structure of the blockchain. Many of these attacks are related to the pooled mining process. Therefore, we first discuss pooled mining and then we will discuss different types of attacks in this category.

Pooled Mining: With the computational power of the Bitcoin network growing, it becomes more difficult for individual miners to mine a new block. Finding a block has a significant reward, but an individual's computational power[1] is minimal compared to the network. Hence, an individual has a tiny chance of

---

[1] Terms '*computational power ratio*' and '*hashrate*' both refer to the ratio of the number of hashes that a miner can generate per unit of time to the total number of hashes that the whole network can generate. We use these two terms interchangeably throughout this paper.

finding a block. Therefore, in this case, the reward variance is very high because most of the time, a solo miner will receive no reward, but on a very rare occasion, she will receive a significant reward.

To reduce income fluctuation, miners usually join forces and create pools to mine together and share the reward. With their hashrates combined, they will find blocks more often and divide the reward among themselves. By doing so, they will reduce the fluctuation of the reward significantly because they will receive smaller rewards but frequently. Obviously, the expected value of the reward for a single miner will not change, and she will receive the same reward in the long run.

Mining Attacks: There are several categories of attacks against the Bitcoin network and other blockchains in general [7,10]. One of these categories is mining attacks. Attacks in this category target the mining process in Bitcoin. These attacks are usually not related to the security of the Bitcoin and Bitcoin network, meaning they are not trying to compromise the validity of the blockchain or steal bitcoins. Instead, they target the miners and pools. In a scenario where all miners are working honestly (loyal to the Bitcoin protocol), in the long run, any miner will receive a reward proportional to her hashrate. For example, suppose that the total hashrate of the entire Bitcoin network is one. Then suppose one miner or a pool of miners have a fraction of it, say α. So, the ratio of the reward for this miner should also be α. We call it the miner's '*fair share*' of the rewards. In mining attacks, attackers try to increase their revenue beyond their fair share and/or decrease other miners' (or pools) revenues [3]. These attacks include selfish mining [9], block withholding attack [23], stubborn mining [18], optimal selfish mining [26], fork after withholding attack [13], coin-hopping attack [16] to name a few.

2.2 Selfish Mining

One of the most famous attacks in this category is '*Selfish Mining*', introduced by Eyal and Sirer [8]. In selfish mining, the attacker (also known as the selfish miner) starts to mine, and if she finds a new block, unlike what the protocol states, she does not publish its block to other miners. Instead, she keeps it for herself and tries to find the next block on top of it. The importance of selfish mining is that it is not limited to Bitcoin, and it can be applied in other blockchains, e.g., Ethereum [11,15,20,22]. Based on [14,28], until now, pools in the Bitcoin network have not been large enough for selfish mining to be profitable, and the only case of selfish mining in the real world has been observed in Monacoin [24]. However, the likelihood of such attacks is increasing with the growth in the Bitcoin network.

Selfish mining is an attack from a mining pool toward other miners or mining pools. Selfish miners do not follow the protocol. Instead, they follow a set of rules that help them waste honest miners' efforts, increasing their proportional reward. Briefly, when a selfish miner/pool finds a block, she will not propagate it immediately but keep it for herself, so other miners cannot mine on the top of her block, which is the last block in the blockchain. By doing so, she creates a private branch alongside the public one (that is accessible by everyone). Then she publishes her private branch whenever it's needed according to a specific set of rules to invalidate honest miners' blocks. This set of rules is called selfish strategy and it indicates which action should be taken by the selfish miner based on the state of the network (length of the branches) and the last event in the network (either the new block is mined by the selfish miner or other miners). By following the selfish strategy, the attacker will waste a lot of computational power from honest miners. There are multiple pieces of research that analyze selfish mining in different circumstances. For example, Negy et al. re-examined selfish mining under different difficulty adjustment algorithms that are used in popular cryptocurrencies [19]. Motlagh et al. analyzed the effect of selfish mining on the performance of the network [17]. Also, several researchers have studied selfish mining in a network with multiple selfish miners [1, 29, 30].

Because of the decentralized nature and anonymity (pseudonymity) of Bitcoin and blockchain, detecting selfish mining is not so straightforward. However, there have been some attempts to detect this attack [5]. For instance, one method of detecting selfish mining has been proposed by Saad et al. [24]. They leveraged the expected transaction confirmation height and the block publishing height to detect selfish mining behaviour in Proof of Work (PoW)-based Blockchains. Using the relationship between the two features, they created a "truth state" for each published block in order to distinguish between a legitimate block and a selfishly mined block.

There are some mitigation methods proposed to prevent mining attacks [21]. Our focus here is on selfish mining prevention. Eyal and Sirer themselves proposed the first mitigation strategy in [9], which suggests a slight change in the Bitcoin protocol. Bitcoin protocol requires that if a node receives two blocks with the same height, it should accept the first one, broadcast it to others, and ignore the second block completely. In this mitigation, They suggest that in this situation, you should broadcast both of those blocks and choose one of them *randomly*. They prove that using this technique will set the minimum hash power required by a selfish miner to 25%. So, it is called a 25% defence against selfish mining because by using this technique, the selfish miner should have at least 25% of the network hash power to benefit from selfish mining.

There have been several attempts to mitigate selfish mining, e.g. Freshness Preferred technique [12], and Zeroblock [27]. However, the problem with these mitigation techniques is that they need significant changes to the Bitcoin protocol. Because of this, the Bitcoin community has not adopted any of them as a solution to be added to the Bitcoin protocol. Also, these solutions do not pay attention to the difficulty adjustment algorithm, which is why selfish mining becomes profitable. We will discuss this in the following sections.

One other proposed solution to this problem is Zeno's DAA [2]. In their work, first, the authors investigated the profitability of selfish mining regarding time. They showed that selfish mining is not profitable at the beginning (the first couple of difficulty adjustment periods) but will eventually become profitable for the attacker. Therefore, every attacker should wait a considerable amount of time for the selfish mining attack to become profitable. So, selfish mining behaviour could be discouraged by extending this waiting time. Then, they proposed a new difficulty adjustment algorithm called Zeno's DAA that could effectively extend this waiting period while keeping the other properties of a good DAA. We will discuss Zeno's DAA in detail in the next section.

One shortcoming of their proposed algorithm is that it treats the increment and decrement of the difficulty value the same. However, we only need to change the decrement of the difficulty to be slower to prevent selfish mining. One of our proposed algorithms tries to tackle this issue by making the difficulty value more sensitive to increasing the difficulty rather than decreasing it.

Another shortcoming of Zeno's is that it cannot be tuned to the specific needs of the blockchain in general or at the moment. For example, one blockchain system might be able to endure longer periods of high average block generation rate, and another one might not. So, in our other proposed algorithm, we made Zeno's DAA parametric, so it can be tuned accordingly.

3   Proposed Approach

First, we have to understand what makes a good difficulty adjustment algorithm. For example, similar to the original Bitcoin difficulty adjustment algorithm, it should be easy to understand, implement, and compute. Everyone should be able to compute it by themselves without any need to interact with others, just by having the blockchain history to this point.

In selfish mining, the attacker's focus is to lower the difficulty of the whole network and gain profit from higher relative revenue. However, the selfish miner has to wait for a while before selfish mining becomes profitable for her. What Zeno's DAA tries to achieve is to propose an alternative DAA that could extend this waiting period to discourage miners from performing selfish mining attacks. This results in a lower block generation rate, and we cannot guarantee a constant block generation rate. However, there will always be a trade-off between allowing miners to perform selfish mining attacks and tolerating a slight decrease in block generation rate. Zeno's aims for the latter while keeping the block generation rate as close to the desired value as possible because we need to keep transaction confirmation time as low as possible.

The formula of Bitcoin's current DAA is as follows:

$$D_n = D_{n-1} \times \frac{2016 \times 600}{t_{b_{2016 \times n}} - t_{b_{2016 \times (n-1)}}} \qquad (1)$$

in which, D_n is the difficulty from the n'th period forward, b_i is the i'th block, and t_{b_i} is the generation time for block i in seconds. Also, the numerator is the expected time for generating 2016 blocks for an average of $600\,\mathrm{s}$ (10 min).

Zeno's DAA modifies the original DAA of Bitcoin to make the difficulty sensitive to history, not just the current period. We formulate it as follows:

$$E_{n-1} = D_{n-1} \times \frac{2016 \times 600}{t_{b_{2016 \times n}} - t_{b_{2016 \times (n-1)}}} \tag{2}$$

$$D_n = \frac{1}{2} E_{n-1} + \frac{1}{2} D_{n-1}. \tag{3}$$

Here, E_{n-1} is the expected difficulty for the previous period, and D_{n-1} is the difficulty value that has been used for this period. But, unlike what the current DAA does, we do not set this value as the next period's difficulty. Instead, we set the difficulty value of the next period as a simple average between the two.

3.1   Zeno's Max

One of the possible downsides of Zeno's DAA is that it gradually changes the difficulty, whether it's decreasing or increasing it. This might be good for the case that we want to extend the waiting period of the selfish mining attack, but in case of scaling the network, it is not desirable.

So, we propose a new difficulty adjustment algorithm by making a simple change in Zeno's DAA to make it somehow asymmetric and more sensitive to increasing the difficulty than decreasing it. Here is the new DAA, called Zeno's Max DAA:

$$E_{n-1} = D_{n-1} \times \frac{2016 \times 600}{t_{b_{2016 \times n}} - t_{b_{2016 \times (n-1)}}}$$

$$D_n = max(E_{n-1}, \frac{1}{2} E_{n-1} + \frac{1}{2} D_{n-1}). \tag{4}$$

As you can see in this formula, it chooses the difficulty value of the next period as the maximum value of E_{n-1}, and an average of E_{n-1} and D_{n-1}. In other words, we can say that Zeno's Max DAA behaves like Zeno's DAA in decreasing the difficulty and behaves like the default DAA in increasing the difficulty. Because in selfish mining, we are only concerned about the difficulty decrease, therefore in regards to selfish mining, it behaves just like Zeno's DAA. However, because it increases the difficulty all the way in one step, it scales the network as fast as the default DAA, which is much faster than Zeno's DAA.

3.2   Zeno's Parametric

Another possible downside of Zeno's DAA is that it only calculates a simple average between E_{n-1} and D_{n-1}. We discussed that Zeno's DAA is trying to make smaller changes than the default DAA to the difficulty value to delay the profitability of selfish mining. The cost of this would be a slightly higher value for block generation time. So, there is a trade-off. In Zeno's DAA, there is no way to tune how much we can tolerate the increase in block generation time to delay the profitability of selfish mining and discourage it. By making Zeno's

DAA parametric, we can overcome this issue. Here is the formula for Zeno's Parametric DAA:

$$E_{n-1} = D_{n-1} \times \frac{2016 \times 600}{t_{b_{2016 \times n}} - t_{b_{2016 \times (n-1)}}}$$

$$D_n = (1 - \tau) \times E_{n-1} + \tau \times D_{n-1}. \tag{5}$$

The parameter here is τ. The acceptable range for this parameter is $[0, 1)$. If τ is 0.5, Zeno's Parametric would be equivalent to Zeno's DAA. On the other hand, if τ is 0, it would be equivalent to the default DAA, as it only includes E_{n-1} and not D_{n-1}.

The parameter τ could be selected based on the specific needs of a blockchain. For example, a particular type of blockchain might be able to tolerate longer periods of higher block generation time but wants to discourage selfish behaviour more. For this blockchain, a higher value of τ might be better, and vice versa.

4 Evaluation and Results

This section evaluates our proposed difficulty adjustment algorithms based on Zeno's DAA, Zeno's Max and Zeno's Parametric. We compare them to Zeno's DAA in terms of scalability of the network and how they respond to network growth and their effects on selfish mining attacks.

4.1 Evaluation Metrics

To be able to analyze difficulty adjustment algorithms, we need some evaluation metrics. The simplest, yet most important, evaluation metric is *total net revenue*. Because it is the most important and very likely the sole factor for miners to participate in Bitcoin mining. The reason for emphasizing the term *total net revenue* is that, as discussed before, there are some cases in which the miners' *relative revenue* will increase. But that is not desired because a miner does not want her total net revenue to decrease, even if her relative revenue increases. Since the number of bitcoins mined is directly related to the number of blocks generated (currently 6.25 bitcoins per block), we simply consider the number of blocks generated by a miner as her total net revenue and denote it as R. Suppose t is the time (in hours) since a particular miner P_i started to mine.

$$R_{P_i}(t): \quad \text{Number of blocks generated by} \tag{6}$$
$$\text{the pool } P_i \text{ in time } t$$
$$\text{(Total net revenue of the pool} P_i)$$

The scenario where all miners are honest is our baseline, which defines our expected value of the revenue. Because in this scenario, every miner will receive its fair share of the total revenue, and any deviation from this amount shows either loss or profit. We denote the revenue in the all-honest scenario as $\overline{R}$ as below.

$$\overline{R}_{P_i}(t) = \alpha_i \times t \times 6 \tag{7}$$

The constant value of 6 in the equation above indicates that, on average, six blocks should be generated by the whole network every hour. In other words, the block generation rate for Bitcoin is ten minutes. For every miner, if all miners are loyal to the protocol (mine honestly), their expected total net revenues are the same as $\overline{R}$ and proportional to their hashrate, α_i.

$$R_{P_i}(t) \approx \overline{R}_{P_i}(t), \text{ if all miners are honest} \tag{8}$$

By comparing R_{P_i} and $\overline{R}_{P_i}$ in the presence of selfish miners, we can see if the configuration of miners has any profit or loss for every miner or not. Therefore we define another metric to see this comparison. It is a normalized gain or loss metric which we call it '*gain*' for short, denote it by G_{P_i} and defined as follows:

$$G_{P_i}(t) = \frac{R_{P_i}(t) - \overline{R}_{P_i}(t)}{t \times 6} \tag{9}$$

In the case of all miners being honest, G_{P_i} should be zero. Because the numerator of the equation above equals zero (as $R_{P_i}(t) \approx \overline{R}_{P_i}(t)$).

4.2   Simulator

We developed and used a simulator to simulate different scenarios and analyze their outcome. Our simulator is a discrete-event simulator. Unlike continuous simulators, it is based on events. In this type of simulation, it is assumed that no changes occur between two consecutive events. So the simulator can jump to the next event and process it. These kinds of simulators are typically faster because they are not required to simulate every time slice.

For implementing other mining strategies, we just have to define different types of miners and implement the policy of the miner on each event under different circumstances. We implemented the strategy described in Sect. 2.2 and used this new miner to analyze the selfish mining attack. After running the simulator for the desired amount of time, we can get the simulation outcome and analyze them to get our desired results.

4.3   Findings

Zeno's Max: For our first scenario, imagine a situation that after one period (right at the beginning of the second period), the network grows by %50. This means that the network difficulty has to be increased by the DAA. Figure 1a shows the difficulty value of the network for the default DAA, Zeno's DAA and Zeno's Max DAA. As can be seen there, at the beginning of the episode (left side of the figure), default DAA and Zeno's Max behave precisely the same and do this increase in one step. However, Zeno's DAA does this in multiple phases, and it takes a lot longer to reach the desired value.

The second event in this scenario is that one miner changes its strategy from honest mining to selfish mining at the beginning of the seventh period. Because of this, the value of difficulty has to decrease to compensate for all those discarded blocks. However, as we discussed before, we want this process to be gradual to extend the waiting time of the selfish mining attackers. Therefore, as it can be seen on the right side of Fig. 1a, this time Zeno's Max behaves similar to Zeno's instead and does this in multiple steps.

Figure 1b shows the average block generation time, and as it can also be seen here, for increasing the block generation time, Zeno's Max acts like the default DAA, and for decreasing it, Zeno's Max act like Zeno's DAA. This make scaling the network faster while extending the waiting time for the selfish miners.

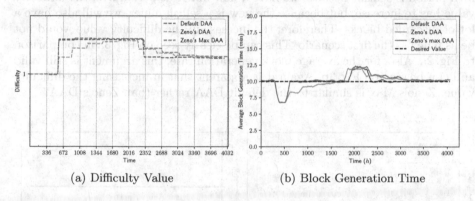

(a) Difficulty Value   (b) Block Generation Time

Fig. 1. Comparison between three DAAs

Now let's take a look at four different scenarios and compare the performance of these three DAAs.

(S_1) Starts with honest miners; Another honest miner joins after five periods.
(S_2) Starts with honest miners; A selfish miner joins after five periods.
(S_3) Starts with a selfish miner in the network; An honest miner joins after five periods.
(S_4) Starts with a selfish miner in the network; Another selfish miner joins after five periods.

Figure 2a and Fig. 2b show the difficulty value and block generation time for the S_1 respectively. It is clear in this scenario that when we need an increase in the value of the difficulty (which directly leads to an increase to the average block generation rate), Zeno's Max and the default DAA behave similarly and do this in one step, in contrast with the Zeno's DAA that does it step by step.

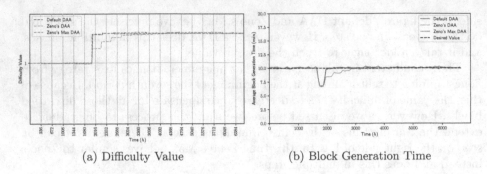

(a) Difficulty Value (b) Block Generation Time

Fig. 2. Comparison between three DAAs in S_1

The second scenario is similar to the first one, but the miner who joins at the fifth period is selfish. Because we have a new miner at period five, the difficulty value has to increase, but because the new is a selfish miner, we will also have a lot of discarded blocks. Therefore, the increase in the difficulty value would not be as much as the first scenario. This can be clearly seen on Fig. 3a in comparison to Fig. 2a. Also, for the average block generation rate, this argument is still valid and can be seen on Fig. 3b. Again it is apparent that in increasing the difficulty value, Zeno's Max is similar to the default DAA rather than Zeno's DAA.

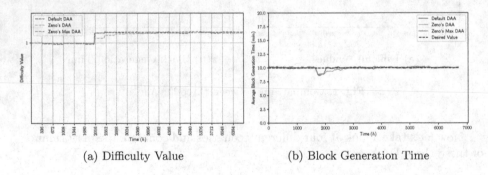

(a) Difficulty Value (b) Block Generation Time

Fig. 3. Comparison between three DAAs in S_2

The following two scenarios, S_3 and S_4, are a bit different from the first two. In these scenarios, we start with a selfish miner. Therefore, in the beginning, the block generation time increases (Fig. 4b and Fig. 5b), and we have to decrease the difficulty to take the block generation time back to its desired value. As shown at the beginning of Fig. 4a and Fig. 5a, the difficulty value will decrease after the first period. However, while reducing the difficulty value, Zeno's Max behaves similarly to Zeno's DAA and gradually reduces the difficulty value. But when the new miner joins the network after period five, it again acts as the default DAA. The difference between S_3 and S_4 is that in S_4, the new miner is also selfish. Because of that, the increment in the difficulty value after period five is not as much as S_3.

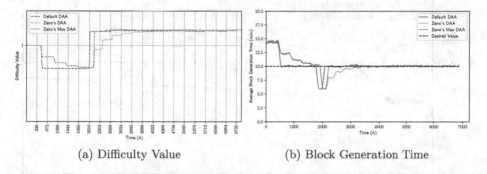

(a) Difficulty Value   (b) Block Generation Time

Fig. 4. Comparison between three DAAs in S_3

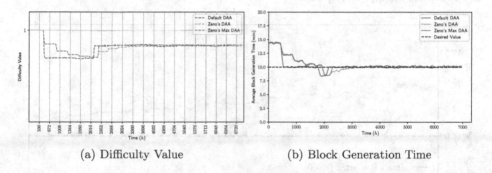

(a) Difficulty Value   (b) Block Generation Time

Fig. 5. Comparison between three DAAs in S_4

Zeno's Parametric: For evaluating this method, we take a look at the behaviour of different values for τ in the same scenario. Figure 6 shows the results of $G(t)$ (gain for the selfish miner) when $\alpha = 0.5$ for different values of τ. It is evident in this figure that for the larger values of τ, the break-even point (the point where the G curve reaches the value of zero) will be delayed more and more.

Figure 7 shows the average block generation time for different values of τ in the same scenario as above. It shows that for larger values of τ, the average block generation time will take longer to return to its intended value (ten minutes). This is the trade-off that we discuss in the previous section. If a blockchain can tolerate more prolonged periods of higher block generation time, it can use a higher value for τ to discourage selfish behaviour more intensively.

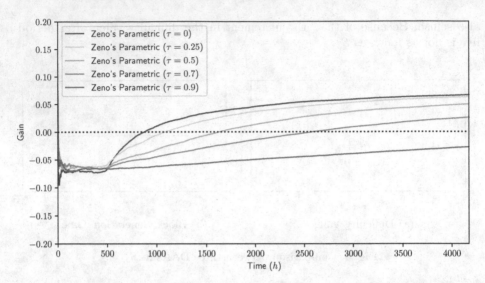

Fig. 6. Gain for a selfish miner with $\alpha = 0.4$ for different values of τ ($\tau = 0$: Default DAA, $\tau = 0.5$: Zeno's DAA)

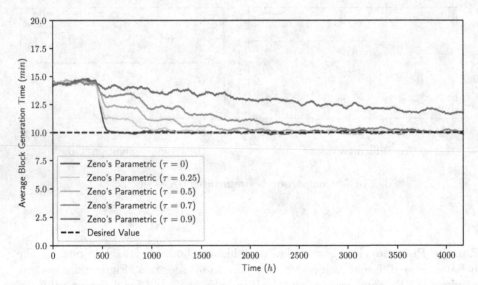

Fig. 7. Block generation time ($\alpha = 0.4$) for different values of τ ($\tau = 0$: Default DAA, $\tau = 0.5$: Zeno's DAA)

In Fig. 8 the values for difficulties with different values of τ are depicted. As it can be seen here, difficulty values decrease step by step. However, by increasing the value of τ, the heights of the steps decrease, and the lengths of them increase.

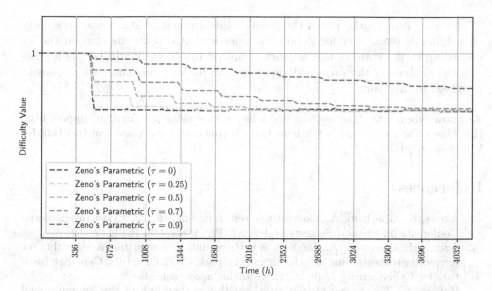

Fig. 8. Difficulty value ($\alpha = 0.4$) for different values of τ ($\tau = 0$: Default DAA, $\tau = 0.5$: Zeno's DAA)

5   Conclusion and Future Work

In this work, we tried to address the issues with Zeno's DAA and improve its performance by introducing two new difficulty adjustment algorithms based on it. In the beginning, we briefly reviewed the literature around the security of bitcoin and selfish mining and why the previous solutions for selfish mining were not so practical. Then we reviewed the properties of a good DAA, and then we proposed two new methods: Zeno's Max and Zeno's Parametric.

In the next section, we evaluated the two new DAAs. The first proposed DAA, Zeno's Max DAA, has an advantage over Zeno's DAA because it treats increment and decrement of the difficulty value differently. It acts like the default DAA for increasing difficulty, and for decreasing the difficulty, it acts like Zeno's DAA. Because of this, Zeno's Max DAA can scale the network much faster than Zeno's while discouraging selfish miners by extending their break-even time.

Our second proposed method, Zeno's Parametric, considers that not every blockchain can tolerate the same amount of higher block generation time. Because of this, we introduced parameter τ to the formula. The value of τ could be from $[0, 1)$. By introducing Zeno's Parametric, default DAA and Zeno's DAA became members of Zeno's Parametric DAAs with $\tau = 0$ and $\tau = 0.5$, respectively. For values closer to zero, the behaviour of the DAA would be closer to the default DAA, meaning the difficulty adjustment will happen in bigger steps and thus faster. Increasing it makes the difficulty adjustment slower, which leads to more waiting time for the selfish miners. However, the block generation time will go back to its intended value later. Zeno's Parametric allows blockchain designers to tune it and find the optimal value for their specific needs.

As our future work, one of the possible directions is to study the possibility of a dynamic parameter for Zeno's Parametric that can be changed on the fly according to the state of the network. Another future work will be the mathematical analysis of the proposed algorithms to back up our simulation analysis provided in this work.

Acknowledgments. The authors graciously acknowledge the funding support from the Tier 1 Canada Research Chair to Dr. Ghorbani, and the Canadian Institute for Cybersecurity (CIC).

References

1. Azimy, H., Ghorbani, A.: Competitive selfish mining. In: 2019 17th International Conference on Privacy, Security and Trust (PST), pp. 1–8. IEEE (2019)
2. Azimy, H., Ghorbani, A., Bagheri, E.: A new difficulty adjustment algorithm for preventing selfish mining attack. Technical report, CIC TR2021-04, Canadian Institute for Cybersecurity (July 2021). [available upon request]
3. Bahack, L.: Theoretical bitcoin attacks with less than half of the computational power (draft). arXiv preprint arXiv:1312.7013 (2013)
4. Berdik, D., Otoum, S., Schmidt, N., Porter, D., Jararweh, Y.: A survey on blockchain for information systems management and security. Inf. Process. Manage. **58**(1), 102397 (2021)
5. Chicarino, V., Albuquerque, C., Jesus, E., Rocha, A.: On the detection of selfish mining and stalker attacks in blockchain networks. Ann. Telecommun. **75**, 143–152 (2020). https://doi.org/10.1007/s12243-019-00746-2
6. Conti, M., Kumar, E.S., Lal, C., Ruj, S.: A survey on security and privacy issues of bitcoin. IEEE Commun. Surv. Tut. **20**(4), 3416–3452 (2018)
7. Courtois, N.T., Bahack, L.: On subversive miner strategies and block withholding attack in bitcoin digital currency. arXiv preprint arXiv:1402.1718 (2014)
8. Eyal, I., Sirer, E.G.: Bitcoin is broken (2013). [Online; Accessed Feb. 2020]
9. Eyal, I., Sirer, E.G.: Majority is not enough: bitcoin mining is vulnerable. In: Christin, N., Safavi-Naini, R. (eds.) FC 2014. LNCS, vol. 8437, pp. 436–454. Springer, Heidelberg (2014). https://doi.org/10.1007/978-3-662-45472-5_28
10. Gervais, A., Karame, G.O., Wüst, K., Glykantzis, V., Ritzdorf, H., Capkun, S.: On the security and performance of proof of work blockchains. In: Proceedings of the 2016 ACM SIGSAC Conference on Computer and Communications Security, pp. 3–16 (2016)
11. Grunspan, C., Pérez-Marco, R.: Selfish mining in Ethereum. arXiv preprint arXiv:1904.13330 (2019)
12. Heilman, E.: One weird trick to stop selfish miners: fresh bitcoins, a solution for the honest miner (poster abstract). In: Böhme, R., Brenner, M., Moore, T., Smith, M. (eds.) FC 2014. LNCS, vol. 8438, pp. 161–162. Springer, Heidelberg (2014). https://doi.org/10.1007/978-3-662-44774-1_12
13. Kwon, Y., Kim, D., Son, Y., Vasserman, E., Kim, Y.: Be selfish and avoid dilemmas: fork after withholding (FAW) attacks on bitcoin. In: Proceedings of the 2017 ACM SIGSAC Conference on Computer and Communications Security, pp. 195–209. ACM (2017)
14. Lee, S., Kim, S.: Detective mining: selfish mining becomes unrealistic under mining pool environment. IACR Cryptol. ePrint Arch. **2019**, 486 (2019)

15. Liu, Y., Hei, Y., Xu, T., Liu, J.: An evaluation of uncle block mechanism effect on Ethereum selfish and stubborn mining combined with an eclipse attack. IEEE Access **8**, 17489–17499 (2020)

16. Meshkov, D., Chepurnoy, A., Jansen, M.: Short paper: revisiting difficulty control for blockchain systems. In: Garcia-Alfaro, J., Navarro-Arribas, G., Hartenstein, H., Herrera-Joancomartí, J. (eds.) ESORICS/DPM/CBT -2017. LNCS, vol. 10436, pp. 429–436. Springer, Cham (2017). https://doi.org/10.1007/978-3-319-67816-0_25

17. Motlagh, S.G.G., Misic, J., Misic, V.B.: The impact of selfish mining on bitcoin network performance. IEEE Trans. Netw. Sci. Eng. **8**, 724–735 (2021)

18. Nayak, K., Kumar, S., Miller, A., Shi, E.: Stubborn mining: generalizing selfish mining and combining with an eclipse attack. In: 2016 IEEE European Symposium on Security and Privacy (EuroS&P), pp. 305–320. IEEE (2016)

19. Negy, K.A., Rizun, P.R., Sirer, E.G.: Selfish mining re-examined. In: Bonneau, J., Heninger, N. (eds.) FC 2020. LNCS, vol. 12059, pp. 61–78. Springer, Cham (2020). https://doi.org/10.1007/978-3-030-51280-4_5

20. Niu, J., Feng, C.: Selfish mining in Ethereum. arXiv preprint arXiv:1901.04620 (2019)

21. Ren, W., Hu, J., Zhu, T., Ren, Y., Choo, K.-K.R.: A flexible method to defend against computationally resourceful miners in blockchain proof of work. Inf. Sci. **507**, 161–171 (2020)

22. Ritz, F., Zugenmaier, A.: The impact of uncle rewards on selfish mining in Ethereum. In: 2018 IEEE European Symposium on Security and Privacy Workshops (EuroS&PW), pp. 50–57. IEEE (2018)

23. Rosenfeld, M.: Analysis of bitcoin pooled mining reward systems. arXiv preprint arXiv:1112.4980 (2011)

24. Saad, M., Njilla, L., Kamhoua, C., Mohaisen, A.: Countering selfish mining in blockchains. In: 2019 International Conference on Computing, Networking and Communications (ICNC), pp. 360–364. IEEE (2019)

25. Saad, M., et al.: Exploring the attack surface of blockchain: a systematic overview. arXiv preprint arXiv:1904.03487 (2019)

26. Sapirshtein, A., Sompolinsky, Y., Zohar, A.: Optimal selfish mining strategies in bitcoin. In: Grossklags, J., Preneel, B. (eds.) FC 2016. LNCS, vol. 9603, pp. 515–532. Springer, Heidelberg (2017). https://doi.org/10.1007/978-3-662-54970-4_30

27. Solat, S., Potop-Butucaru, M.: ZeroBlock: preventing selfish mining in bitcoin. arXiv preprint arXiv:1605.02435 (2016)

28. Wang, C., Chu, X., Yang, Q.: Measurement and analysis of the bitcoin networks: a view from mining pools. arXiv preprint arXiv:1902.07549 (2019)

29. Zhang, S., Zhang, K., Kemme, B.: Analysing the benefit of selfish mining with multiple players. In: 2020 IEEE International Conference on Blockchain (Blockchain), pp. 36–44. IEEE (2020)

30. Zhang, S., Zhang, K., Kemme, B.: A simulation-based analysis of multiplayer selfish mining. In: 2020 IEEE International Conference on Blockchain and Cryptocurrency (ICBC), pp. 1–5. IEEE (2020)

From Bitcoin to Solana – Innovating Blockchain Towards Enterprise Applications

Xiangyu Li, Xinyu Wang, Tingli Kong, Junhao Zheng, and Min Luo[✉]

Georgia Institute of Technology, Atlanta, GA 30332, USA
mluo60@gatech.edu

Abstract. This survey presents a comprehensive study of recent advances in blockchain technologies, focusing on how issues that affecting the enterprise adoption were progressively addressed from the original Bitcoin system to Ethereum, to Solana etc. Key issues preventing the wide adoption are scalability and performance, while recent advances in Solana has clearly demonstrated that it is possible to significantly improve on those issues by innovating on data structure, processes and algorithms by consolidating various time-consuming algorithms and security enforcements, and differentiate and balance users and their responsibilities and rights, while maintaining the required security and integrity that blockchain systems inherently offer.

Keywords: Blockchain · Distributed ledger · Consensus · Proof of work · Proof of history scalability · Performance · Security

1 Introduction

1.1 Rise of Blockchain Technology

The blockchain is a purely distributed peer-to-peer system of ledgers that utilizes some well-articulated software constructs of algorithms, collaboratively peers to record and negotiate the informational content of ordered and connected blocks of transaction data together with cryptographic and security enrichments to achieve integrity. It was first introduced by Bitcoin in 2009 and has been becoming a mainstream technology. It has been used in various industries, such as financial, healthcare, supply chain, logistics, and many others. Such distributed ledgers are designed to provide a permanent, tamper-proof record of business transactions, as they can be utilized to improve collaboration, enable provenance, speed up transaction settlements or enable transparency.

Blockchain can also be viewed as a decentralized database running on a peer-to-peer network, where each node/computer (or some selected group) maintains a copy of the current ledger. It offers data security and reliability as the data cannot be easily modified while the redundant copies make data loss unlikely.

Blockchain innovated in how digital information is stored, verified and exchanged, and was inherently designed and developed to create secure, reliable and transparent business processes for enterprises. One of the surveys reveals that the global blockchain

K. Lee and L.-J. Zhang (Eds.): ICBC 2021, LNCS 12991, pp. 74–100, 2022.
https://doi.org/10.1007/978-3-030-96527-3_6

market size is expected to grow from USD 4.9 billion in 2021 to USD 67.4 billion in 2026, at a CAGR of 68.4% [47]. As organizations have started to explore and experiment with blockchain's potential by developing blockchain applications, the proper choice of a "good" blockchain platform becomes vital. As they become increasingly more popular, enterprises need better information to make right judgement calls to decide not only when to jump into the tech wagon, but more importantly how they can take advantage of the new technology while avoiding potential pitfalls.

Blockchain and smart contracts make it possible for multiple parties to share business logic and collaboratively conduct business processes/operations automatically. Properly utilized, it can reduce IT costs, expand B2B and B2C networks, enable new products and service that could bring in revenue and profits. Moreover, blockchain's business value is expected to increase as enterprise implementations proliferate and are further extended and refined.

1.2 Issues Facing Enterprise Adoption of Blockchain Technology

This paper will not cover whether blockchain technology fits enterprises from the business perspective, although that should be the first question to ask. We will focus on non-functional requirements that describes the system's operation capabilities and constraints that enhance its business functionality. The non-functional requirements needed for application will of course depend on the business context and the outcomes to be achieved, particularly as there are so many that can be applied. In this paper, we will only elaborate a few most critical ones.

Performance. All enterprise systems should be designed and built with an acceptable standard of performance as a minimum, while taking into accounts problems such as scalability, latency, load and resource utilization. Many factors could negatively impact performance, including high numbers of API calls, poor caching, and high-load third-party services. It's critical to ensure the end-user experience or integration of multi-systems across the entire eco-chain is not affected by any such issues.

Prevailing business transaction systems have been capable of processing thousands (Visa, for example) or millions of transactions (online market place such as Amazon or Alibaba) per second without any failure, most of the current blockchain platforms depicted a remarkable slowdown, making them unviable for large-scale or performance-sensitive applications. For example, Bitcoin can only process roughly 3 to 7 transactions per second, with Ethereum about 15 to 20 transactions.

Such poor performance and cumbersome operations are mainly due to the complexity with encrypted and distributed nature in blockchains. Although it is not at all suitable for high-frequency transactions, ways to improve its transaction performance, including throughput and latency, is always a hot topic. Compared to "traditional" payment systems such as cash or debit cards, it could take hours or even days to process some transactions. When more users join the network, its performance will be further degraded due to the existence of consensus latency from nodes with low processing power. As a result, the transactions cost is higher than usual, further limiting more users onto the network.

Scalability. Scalability is the second big issue that needs to be addressed, as this is one of the core reasons why organizations still hesitate to adopt blockchains.

The system must be able to accommodate ever-increasing volumes (number of users/devices/integrated applications, data and throughput) over time, and is able to scale up and down quickly as the number of users change drastically, as needed.

Security and Integrity. Requirements such as confidentiality, authentication and integrity ensure that valuable (private and confidential) information is protected. Blockchain benefits primarily derive from the trust it fosters, its built-in privacy, security and data integrity and its transparency, as it incorporates a flow of data from complex mathematical operations that cannot be changed once created without being detected, and every transaction is encoded and connected, and therefore it is significantly more reliable than traditional journal methods. This unchangeable and incorruptible characteristic inherently make blockchains safer and better protected against tampering and hacking of information.

Various software engineering tactics can be employed to safeguard valuable/transactional data at many integration points. System architects need to understand legal and compliance requirements and communicate these clearly to the development team, so that the necessary levels of security can be established and enforced jointly.

With blockchains, an external audit can be provided from the distributed ledger. This will inherently enhance privacy and avoid corruption, and help confirm the legitimacy of transactions and offer indisputable proof of transactions.

Availability/Reliability/Resilience. The system must be available for use, and the downtime must be reduced to an acceptable level under any circumstances. For example, mechanisms to avoid single points of failures, and adequate timeouts could be used to enhance system availability and reliability.

Feasibility. Feasibility considers issues such as technology maturity, time-to-market, total cost of ownership, technical knowledge, and migration requirements. Commercial-off-the-shelf (COTS) solutions, managed services and cloud-native functions where appropriate, and close collaboration with development partners with suitable architecture and solution components and services will definitely help address those issues.

This paper surveyed several important blockchain platforms covering the years of evolution from the original Bitcoin system to the more advanced recent offerings. Hopefully, with the information we collected and analyzed, it could help enterprises to make better decisions, while also directs new players where to innovate in order to make blockchain well fit into most enterprises business needs. We will review the chosen frameworks, especially their data structures, processes and algorithms involved in creating a new transaction record (block), and how conflicts or disputes could be resolved in Sect. 2. We will also raise concerns on several key issues related to the afore-mentioned NFRs, especially the performance and scalability. Section 3 then proceeds to analyze the selected platforms and discuss, from the evolutionary nature of blockchain technology since its inception, how critical issues such as performance, and scalability etc. were addressed, especially the most recent advances from Solana, where 2−4 order of magnitude of improvements has been proved possible. Section 4 will first present a quick summary view on how enterprises could leverage the information collected and analyzed in the maker to choose "better-fit" platforms, then points to some remaining issues that should be further evolved or even revolutionized to truly meet some fundamental NFR requirements for enterprise adoption. Some alternative approaches to achieve the secure and immutable nature of the distributed ledger is also included. Section 5 conclude the paper with a few quick remarks.

2   Main Frameworks and Consensus Algorithms

This section will give a general description of blockchain architecture, in terms of how blocks are structured and organized into a chain. Issues related to consensus, performance, and scalability will be explored respectively. The reasons for choosing these five platforms as examples, including Bitcoin, Ethereum, Hyperledger Fabric, EOS and Solana, will be explained at the end of this section.

2.1   General Description of Blockchain and Its Main Data Structure

Blockchain is a chain linking or "chaining" different blocks, while a block is the foundation and formed by recording and calculating all the transactions in a Merkle tree and adding the previous block header hash value(s) into the current header, as in Fig. 1.

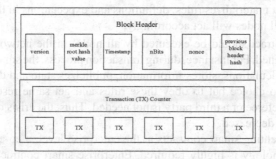

Fig. 1. Block structure

The hash value of the previous block will be included in the current block hash. Figure 2 shows how one block is connected to the other. Note that the first block only has the hash value from its own transactions [1].

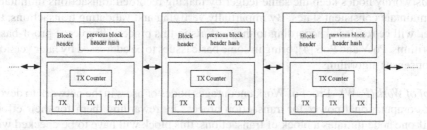

Fig. 2. Chain of block bodies

The main body of each block is structured as a Merkle Tree in Fig. 3, where every transaction is first hashed individually and its hash value is then hashed with another hash value.

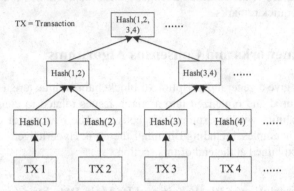

Fig. 3. Merkle Tree inside block body

Smart Contract. In blockchain network, the smart contract is "a secure and unstoppable computer program representing an agreement that is automatically executable and enforceable" [2]. It materializes rules, definitions and expectations in the forms of code and data, so that all nodes will act accordingly.

The smart contract should be executed by all nodes in the network and the same results can be obtained. For instance, during transaction process, the smart contract inside nodes performs calculations, stores information, publicizes state and does transferring. Every node has no choice but to obey these rules and get same results. Under such circumstances, a referee or a third party is not needed. Thus, the crisis of trust inside the network is largely decreased.

When implementing smart contracts at the enterprise level, a co-evolution of both contract and technology is highly required. Enterprise smart contracts can provide a series of service by modularizing data, contract participants and external dependencies [3]. These services can perfectly satisfy the requirements of privacy, scalability and internal administration. More values can be realized in smart contracts with shared and cross-organizational environments that could be enabled by blockchain technology.

Consensus Issues. The consensus algorithm is a mechanism that ensure all distributed untrustworthy nodes keep the same ledger by making recorded transactions immutable and maintain consistent states. By impartially verifying and validating transactions, the nodes will be rewarded according to their efforts in this process. Two core proof-based algorithms, PoW and PoS [4], bring in some basic issues to be addressed by later versions of consensus algorithms.

Proof of Work (PoW). Proof of Work encourages nodes or users in the network to devote their computational power for transaction process by rewarding them for their efforts [5]. If one node initiates a block of transactions, this block will have to be checked with computations by all other nodes, the so called mining process while the participating nodes are miners. Miners will contain a nonce when working out a hash value. This value will eventually be tried out by adjusting nonce and thus a block is validated.

Such consensus mechanism will cause huge waste of computing resource. The whole network of miners will spend their best effort in working out only one hash value. Except the miner who first works it out and gets rewarded, other miners only just wastes their computing power. The efficiency of the mechanism is also low. The time for the mining process would be around 10 min with only one output, etoo low for the real-world business transactions.

Proof of Stake (PoS). Proof of Stake is based on the amount of balance each miner possesses. As many miners may find validated blocks easier with comparatively more computing ability, PoS is designed by rewarding miners with interests based on the amount they own [6]. Their possessions are the "stakes", and it is the stake that decide who will mine the following blocks. There is no competition among miners, and therefore computational waste is reduced to some extent.

However, this mechanism is unreliable. As interests will be rewarded, some miners will large amount of stake might be unwilling to contribute their computational ability and rely only on stakes. This is negative trend that will give rise to lower mobility of transactions.

Performance Issues. From a technical point of view, the typical blockchain network, such as Bitcoin and Ethereum, requires consensus from all nodes in the whole network. Even if a node completes its validation process, it has to wait for consents from other nodes. For Bitcoin, the throughput rate is 7 transactions per second (TPS) and the confirmation time is 60 min. Ethereum blockchain has a better performance with dozens TPS. Such throughput cannot satisfy large-scale enterprise applications. This issue will be even more acute when more users/nodes join the network.

Scalability Issues. The processing power of individual nodes largely determines the scalability of the blockchain system. For instance, when it comes to Bitcoin and Ethereum, each core node in the network that participates in maintenance should maintain a complete storage and be processed.

Many other issues also impact the maturity and the adoption of the blockchain technology, including security and privacy, interoperability, availability and resilience, etc. However as indicated earlier, this paper will focus on the above more critical non-functional related requirements.

2.2 Types of Blockchain Platforms

As more businesses look for adopting blockchain technology, various blockchain platforms have been developed that can be categorized by how open or closed they allow participants contribute to business transactions or verify the accuracy of each block added to the blockchain and the distributed ledger.

All types of blockchains can be characterized as permissionless, permissioned, or both. Permissionless blockchains allow any user to pseudo-anonymously join the blockchain network with full rights, while permissioned blockchains restrict access and also rights to certain nodes. Permissionless blockchains tend to be more secure and reliable than permissioned blockchains, while permissioned blockchains tend to be more efficient, as access to the network is restricted with fewer nodes on the blockchain system.

Table 1. Summarized key features and pros/cons of the four types.

	Public	Private	Consortium	Hybrid
Perminssion	Permissionless	Permissioned	Permissioned	Both
Advantage	Independece	Access control	Access control	Access control
	Transparency	Performance	Security	Performance
	Trust	Scalability	Scalability	Scalability
				Limited independence and transparency
Diadvantage	Performance: long validation times	Security & Trust: more vulnerable to fraud and bad actors	Transparency	Transparency
	Scalability	Auditability	Improved security & trust	Upgrading
	Security			
Typical use cases	Cryptocurrency	Supply chain	Banking	Medical
	Doc validation	Asset ownership	Research	Real estate
			Supply chain	
Example chains	Bitcoin Litecoin	Ripple: virtual currency exchange network	R3: financial services	BM food trust: whole food supply chain
	Ethereum	Hyperledger: General open-source blockchain applications	CargoSmart - Global Shipping Business Network Consortium, shipping industry	

Public (permissionless) blockchain opens to ALL, while not requiring any permission to join. Its consensus process involves all nodes that makes data verification very tedious and time consuming, but it also make the system less vulnerable to hacking or control by a dominant actor. Cryptocurrency uses such chains.

Private (permissioned, managed) blockchain runs on a private network and could be controlled by a single organization, the central authority. It also has the same peer-to-peer architecture as public blockchain, but with significantly reduced scale and therefore better performance. But due to the nature of central/control node(s), its trust is weaker than public blockchains. Security could also be weaker because a small number of nodes could easily decide the consensus used to validate transactions, negating the original intention of the blockchains. Many early blockchain deployments use private blockchains.

Hybrid blockchain combines the features of public and private chains. Such a chain is controlled by a single organization, but with some oversight performed by the public blockchain. It can be used to partition some data and transactions behind a permission scheme while maintaining connections to the public chains. By not allowing the owner to modify transaction data, the security and data integrity risks of private blockchain can be alleviated with potentially better performance than public chains.

Consortium blockchain is similar to private blockchains. It is controlled by a group instead of a single entity, therefore less security susceptible than private chains.

2.3 Why We Choose the Six Platforms?

This paper is about innovating blockchain technology for enterprise adoption that could revolutionize how businesses can take advantages of the inherent secure information exchange and transaction integrity, and make the end-to-end integration of cross-border, organizations and business units seamless, driven and managed by agreed upon contracts that can be automatically executed with trust-worthy results. As the number and quality of blockchain platforms with enterprise-class development tools and architectures has reached a point where most companies can find a suitable platform and supportive community of developers and system integrators, it is still essential to understand their underlying technology stack and related algorithms, their relative merits, in order to find the best possible match for future business growth.

After analyzing almost every available blockchain platforms in the current market place, we selected six, 2 representatives, Bitcoin and Ethereum, for mostly public blockchain; and 2 Hyperledger Fabric and EOS, for private or alliance chains. Number 5 is R3 Corda, a non-traditional blockchain based distributed ledger. The most recent news regarding some very innovative mechanisms introduced in Solana boasted a 2+ order of magnitude improvements on TPS, and we believe that it is really the perfect Number 6 that not only promising, but more importantly evidence that basic blockchain structures and algorithms could still be significantly innovated to serve as the foundation of many enterprise applications. Figure 4 shows the evolution timeline of the five platforms.

Bitcoin and Ethereum are the top 2 well-known public blockchain platforms. Bitcoin is the first realization of blockchain and brings in consensus algorithms in a peer-to-peer system. Ethereum modify the traditional bitcoin structure by successfully implementing accounts and smart contracts. However, these public blockchains have their deficits in scalability and performance.

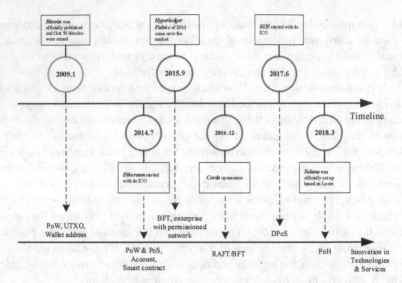

Fig. 4. Development of blockchain platforms

Under such circumstances, the private blockchain and consortium blockchain come into sight. Hyperledger Fabric and EOS are two enterprise blockchain platforms. In these permissioned networks, not all the nodes are equal peers – consensus verifying work is allocated among a small group of members. The consensus algorithms will also be less complicated than those in the public blockchain.

R3 Corda is a representative directed-acyclic-graph based distributed ledger with similar security and immutability as in basic blockchains (Bitcoin, Ethereum), but also better performance.

As mentioned, one of the latest blockchain platform with exciting news is Solana [7]. Solana considerably exceled in terms of its high transaction performance with improved consensuses. Hopefully, if Solana is adopted in enterprise blockchain instead of the existing platforms like Hyperledger Fabric and EOS, the company efficiency can be considerably increased.

Nevertheless, blockchain technology is still under development and man limitations are still need to be further exploited and ameliorated. We will discuss these possibilities in the following sections.

3   Analysis of the Selected Main Frameworks

3.1   Bitcoin

Bitcoin was first designed to replace the use of "cash" in our real world, rather than for the enterprise-level system. Therefore, the concept of "wallet address" (or "wallet") is introduced. This is because Satoshi Nakamoto, the inventor, referenced the model of e-cash when designing the model. It is thus easy to understand that like cash can be put in many places, a Bitcoin user can have many wallets/addresses, with all amounts of balance inside each adding up to the total. These amounts of balance are called "unspent transaction outputs" (UTXO).

UTXO comes from inputs of transactions [8]. However, every input of UTXO is a separate entity which must be used up at a time. Multiple inputs can be inserted in to an address, while up to two outputs can be initiated each time, one for a targeted receiver, the other for getting back the remaining bitcoins. Also, a transfer can be initiated by changing UTXO's current address into the receiver's address. Only the sender with the private key can have access and transfer its UTXO to another address [9]. With UTXO, a transaction in Bitcoin network is just the change of balance's address.

Figure 5 shows how different components of the Bitcoin system work in a transaction process. Before a transaction, network must verify from the previous record whether the sender has enough balance to send. After the validation from all miners (validators) in the whole network, only the first miner who figure out the output is rewarded.

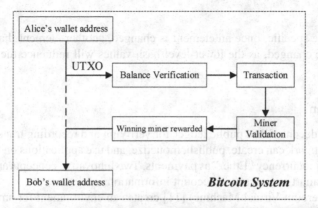

Fig. 5. Bitcoin system components

The above-mentioned transaction is recorded in transaction records. However, in Bitcoin, one deficit with transaction history is apparent: increased verification complexity. When one transaction is initiated, at most two members' previous transactions will be verified – one member is the receiver and the other is the sender. These two members will be traced back for previous transaction records for the amounts of balance in their wallets. As time passes by, the transaction records have been accumulating, and the verification process will be more and more complicated.

This case above is only a one-transaction scenario. If more nodes are added to Bitcoin, when doing transactions, transaction records from more nodes will be considered for calculating balance of a single node, and this will also increase verification complexity.

During transactions process, any changes to the transaction record is prohibited, otherwise the whole chain will be considered invalid. Theoretically, there are up to 5 illegal changes: data content change, Merkle-tree reference change, transaction substitution, Merkle-root change and block-header reference change [10].

The detection of changes is realized by checking changes in block header hash values. In Fig. 6, we denote Transaction 1 to 4 as a part of the Merkle tree. If transaction 2 is changed or replaced, the value of R2 will also change, which will lead to the change in R12 and R34.

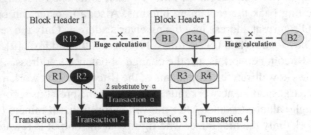

Fig. 6. Bitcoin illegal changes

To be more specific, once an element is changed, another element that points to it should also be changed, as the lower-level hash values will influence the higher-level ones.

3.2 Ethereum

Ethereum is a decentralized public ledger for verifying and recording transactions. The users of the network can create, publish, monetize, and use applications on the platform, and use its cryptocurrency "Ether" as payments. Two innovative concepts are introduced to Ethereum, smart contracts and account information.

EVM (Ethereum Virtual Machine) [11] creates an environment for smart contracts and makes it possible for anyone to create his own contracts and decentralized applications (DApps) [12]. This involves the definition of ownership rules, transaction methods and state transition functions. Smart contracts can further be expanded into business and enterprise level. The codes and data inside represent principles and rules that can be used to provide services according to different scenarios. Several factors can be taken into account, such as internal management, member conducts, privacy etc.

Besides, account [13] is also successfully implemented. There are two sorts of accounts in Ethereum: External Owned Accounts (EOA) [13] and Contract Accounts (CA) [13]. EOA is an e-cash account which encompass balance; while CA has both balance state and contract state. With accounts, the state information, such as balance of users, can be digitalized. This omits the needs to trace back transaction history for balance as in Bitcoin.

Ethereum transactions are validated data that an external account sends to another account [14]. There are three types of transactions: transactions that transfer value between two EOAs; transactions that send a message call to a contract; and transactions that deploy a contract. As all miners are rewarded in a transaction, Gas [15], which can be converted into Ether later, is introduced to restrict the usage of resources. Specifically, to take environment factors into account, such as bandwidth, computational complexity and storage space, Gas value is adjusted after current transaction for the next one.

Figure 7 shows how the above smart contracts and account states are used in the transaction [16]. Before a new transaction starts, gas value is decided based on Ethereum network conditions. As Fig. 7 depicts, Alice first initiate the transaction and then broadcast the whole network. This transaction is added to a block and then miners begin validating. Every miner is reward for its effort with Gas, the amount of which depends on contributions in validating a block.

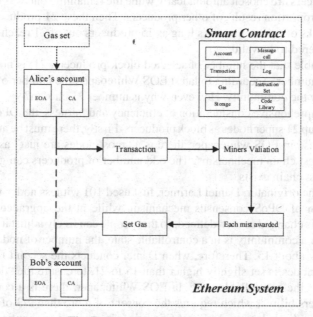

Fig. 7. Ethereum transactions adding

3.3 EOS

EOS (Enterprise Operation System) is a blockchain-based operating system which provides a platform for the development of secure and scalable decentralized applications (DApps) [17]. It provides databases, account permissions, scheduling, authentication and Internet application communication, which greatly improves the efficiency of intelligent business development.

EOS provides not only tools for DApps, but also solutions for scalability issues, which we will further discuss in Sect. 3.5. EOS has the following three main features [18]:

1. Low latency. The platform supports low latency with DPoS mechanism.
2. Parallel Performance. The off-load can allocated among multiple CPUs and computers in terms of large-scale applications. This avoid heavy on-chain workload.
3. Sequential Performance. Due to some limitations in sequentially dependent steps, those applications that cannot support parallel algorithms will be provided with fast sequential processing for high volumes.

By deploying DPoS (Delegated Proof of Stake) consensus mechanism [19], this permissioned EOS blockchain has become suitable for not only public occasions, but also private enterprise cases. The most representative enterprise cases include:

DPOS is an improved version of PoS for permissioned purposes. DPOS selects nodes (block producers) as representatives to partake in later transaction validation work [20]. At the initial stage of each round, a total of 21 block producers are selected (voted), among which 20 producers are chosen automatically while the remaining one was chosen based on the voting proportion results of other producers. Then these 21 producers will begin to validate blocks of transactions. As long as 15 producers out of 21 reach consensus, a block is considered to be valid.

It is noticeable that the number of selected block producers, 21, is not an absolute unchangeable number. According to latest EOS Whitepaper, the number of super nodes can be voted by the community. However, why is number 21 chosen?

For the comprehensive consideration of efficiency and fairness, the DPoS consensus mechanism set up 21 super nodes as block producers. Firstly, there must be an odd number of nodes, because in EOS whitepaper, there is a "most nodes are just" assumption, as well as a "longest chain mechanism". The odd number of producers can guarantee that only one longest chain exists.

Secondly, the originator, Daniel Larimer, first used 101 witness nodes when making the first version of DPoS consensus mechanism, while in the upgraded version, the number of 101 is changed to user-defined, so that people can freely adjust it when voting. However, when a community is in a controllable state, the number of nodes that can be voted is usually about 15. Therefore, when Daniel conducts the second DPoS project, the number of nodes is set slightly higher than 15 to 21, to ensure the "decentralized" operation under the controllable state. In EOS Whitepaper, there is a confirmation of "absolute irreversibility", which requires the consent of more than 2/3 of the nodes. If the number of nodes is large, a longer waiting time is required for confirmation. If the number of nodes is small, shorter waiting time is prone to some concentration risks. It is understandable that 21 is a balance between decentralization and performance.

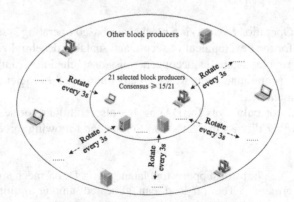

Fig. 8. Hyperledger Fabric architecture

There is also rotation mechanism in the selection of producers: every three seconds, the 21 producers are selected from all producers again. This means producers without enough computing power will be sifted out. With no peer competition and shorter consensus confirmation time, it is possible for EOS to improve its scalability and performance of TPS in each unit time [21]. In Fig. 8, the principles of DPoS and the rotation.

Especially in a company, this small-scale permissioned stake mechanism allows only some directors, similar to the 21 selected block producers, to have the right in the income, property, copyrights etc. in proportion to investment or token in the account [21]. This can strengthen the administration inside an organization.

3.4 Hyperledger Fabric

Hyperledger is a project of open source blockchains to support collaborative development of blockchain- based distributed ledgers. Among them, Hyperledger Fabric is a permissioned blockchain system which aims to build a foundational blockchain platform for enterprises. It provides a modularized framework for enterprises and supports authority management and data security. The two most distinct improvements brought by Hyperledger Fabric are efficiency and confidentiality.

Hyperledger Fabric first introduces the blockchain technology for enterprise use. Compared with blockchain technology, the advantages of Hyperledger Fabric are reflected in the increase in performance and strength on confidentiality. The Hyperledger Fabric architecture is shown in Fig. 9.

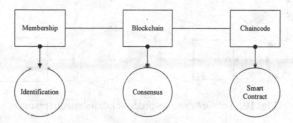

Fig. 9. Hyperledger Fabric architecture

There are three main components in Hyperledger Fabric: Membership, Blockchain and Chaincode. Membership part provides identification services. Blockchain part provides consensus services. Chaincode part is a program that acts as smart contracts in this system. In enterprise scenarios, each node could access this system through the membership services.

The network is permissioned because the participants are known to each other, rather than anonymous and therefore fully untrusted. This is the most distinct difference from the traditional public permissionless Bitcoin and Ethereum blockchain system. The whole system could use general-purpose programming languages such as Java, Go and Node.js, rather than constrained domain-specific languages. However, this uniform programming style and the strict identification process also limit the scalability of the whole system [22].

There are many smart contracts in this system and each maintains a specific type of transaction. Different smart contracts are in charge of different types of transactions. The smart contract will assign endorsers in a specific type of transaction. The endorser is a node which is qualified to validate this specific transaction. The smart contract could also set requirements of completing some specific transaction. For example, it could stipulate that a transaction is completed with validation from 2/3 of endorsers.

When a transaction is initiated, some specific smart contracts will be triggered. Then this transaction will be sent to relevant endorser nodes, which will endorse this transaction. If this transaction is validated, then the result will be directly sent to the user, but not committed on the chain. In this way, the transaction is executed before being validated by the system. Finally, all the transactions, no matter successful or not, will be gathered by the order node for the validation of the whole system. This "execute-order-validate" mechanism is shown in Fig. 10.

This "execute-order-validate" mechanism greatly improves the performance and scalability of the whole system. This first phase also eliminates any non-determinism, as inconsistent results can be filtered out before ordering. Because we have eliminated non-determinism, Fabric is the first blockchain technology that enables use of standard programming languages, which in turn improves the extensibility and scalability of the system. The highest TPS of Fabric could reach 20000 [23].

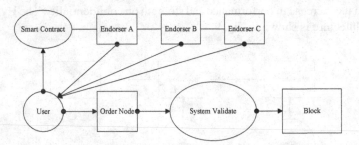

Fig. 10. Fabric "execute-order-validate" mechanism

Another attractive attribute of Fabric is the high confidentiality. The lack of confidentiality can be problematic for many enterprise-use cases, because it is impossible to maintain business relationships in a completely transparent network. Hyperledger Fabric enables confidentiality through its channel architecture and private data feature. The system could set the availability of specific data by assigning authorized peers. The assignment of confidentiality is shown in Fig. 11.

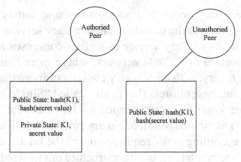

Fig. 11. Fabric confidentiality

3.5 R3 Corda

R3 Corda [24] was developed to make it easier to record and process financial transactions. It uses a peer-to-peer model in which each peer stores data that relates to all the transactions it has participated in. Consequently, re-creating an audit trail requires querying multiple nodes involved in a chain of transactions. This approach can secure data about transactions by securing the appropriate set of peers. Corda simplifies the creation, automation and enforcement of smart contracts -- a key application of blockchain -- compared to DAG-based distributed ledger technologies. In addition, the Iota Foundation just announced an alpha version of the Iota Smart Contracts Protocol, which could provide functions similar to Corda's.

There are two types of membership in Corda: working node and notary node [25]. The working nodes are in charge of ledger recording as in Blockchain and Ethereum. The notary nodes are trusted by involved parties of transaction and can provide validation of effective transactions. Each notary node is connected with a database or a database cluster. The "effective" here means a certain input data has not been or is not becoming the input of other transactions to ensure that there is no "double spending" issue. Corda is a "permissioned" global network. One working node can be connected to different notary nodes in different transactions, and only involved parties (nodes) will have access and maintain the data of a transaction. Notary nodes will ensure effective transactions and prevent "double spending" issue.

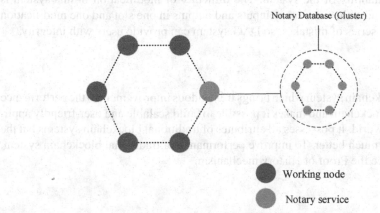

Fig. 12. Single notary network

There are multiple notary nodes in a notary service to satisfy the requirement of consensus and finally figure out the decision. These notary services are decentralized – each group may have its own notary service as well as consensus algorithm. Shown in Fig. 12 is the basic structure of a Corda network, where more than one working node may be connected to a notary, with each notary consists of more than one notary nodes, consisting of a notary database cluster. This is also called "Single Notary Network".

There are two other kinds of notary service model in Corda: "Clustered Multiple Notary Network" and "Distributed Multiple Notary Network". Different types of notary network are deployed according to the requirements of the financial enterprise system.

DAG, directed acyclic graph [26], is a data structure put forward to improve the TPS of blockchain system. The traditional blockchain consensus mechanism is choosing the longest chain. However, DAG consensus mechanism is choosing the heaviest chain.

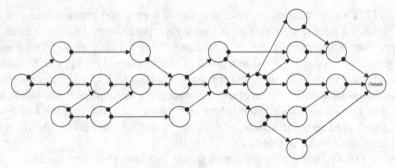

Fig. 13. Directed acyclic graph

As we can see in Fig. 13, each slot can have more than one legal transaction, and every legal transaction can be verified and added into this system. So, the DAG system can save much time spent on synchronization in traditional blockchain system, because DAG system needn't to synchronize. Considering there can be repeated transactions in each slot, the improvement on TPS is not linear, but implementing this DAG data structure can improve the efficiency of the whole system. The nature of asynchronization also extends the scalability of the system. The difficulty of modification in this system is tremendous because there are many inputs and outputs in one slot and one modification can introduce a series of mistakes, so DAG system can provide users with integrity.

3.6 Solana

Solana is a blockchain system which brings tremendous improvement to the performance of traditional blockchain and makes it possible to build scalable and user-friendly applications for the world. It possesses all attributes of traditional blockchain systems but the performance is much better. To improve performance of traditional blockchain system, Solana introduce the Proof of History mechanism.

In Solana system There are two kinds of nodes: Leader and Verifier. The Leader is an elected Proof of History generator, and Solana rotates leaders at fixed intervals. The components of Solana are shown in Fig. 12 The leader will receive the transactions coming from users and order them into a Proof of History sequence.

Proof of History is a mechanism used in Solana. The Proof of History sequence is a list of transactions. The transactions are prearranged by a "Leader", and the timestamp is embodied in this data structure. Every event has a unique hash and account along this data structure. As a function of real time, this information tells us what event had come before another. For example, if we want to know the hash value when index is 300, the only way is to run this algorithm 300 times. We can know that there is real time elapsing in this process from this specific data structure. Time cannot be faked and the future can also not be forecasted. In this way, this system will no longer need to waste computing resources on synchronizing time, because time is preconfigured and unchangeable (Fig. 14).

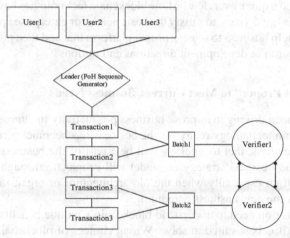

Fig. 14. Components of Solana

Then, transactions will be broken into batches. For example, if the leader wants to send 100 transactions to 10 nodes, it would break 100 transactions into 10 batches and send one to each node. This allows the leader to put 100 transactions on the wire, not 100 transactions for each node. Each node then shares its batch with its peers to reconstruct the original collection of 100 transactions. The process of synchronization between verifiers is shown in Fig. 13. The combination of Proof of history and horizon scaling can improve the performance tremendously [27] (Fig. 15)

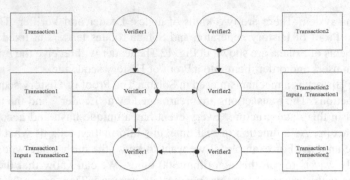

Fig. 15. Verifier synchronization

4   Innovating Blockchain Technology for Enterprise Applications

Section 3 presented a quick overview on how blockchain technologies have been evolved, especially over the last 5 years, to satisfy the basic needs for enterprise applications. This section will first help business to select a proper platform that and then proceed to discuss some further research & development directions and options.

4.1   Select "Best Proper" to Meet Current Business Needs

Technology has been driving to improve business productivity in almost every industry. But whether certain technology really fits the business has become increasingly critical as it is almost inevitable that technology will be a part of the business or its solution. Any change in the business strategy or model will propagate through the company's technology paradigm especially when the old architecture or organizational structure could not support the new business paradigm.

Every organization need to understand blockchain's unique benefits and focus only on problems that it is best suited to solve. Wrong choices of blockchain platforms can carry significant risks, as they could incur project cost overruns and delays, and miss the opportunity for potential benefits. Table 1 provided some quick guidelines on how to make a "wise" selection.

Business Model Drives the Solution. Blockchain platform will drive the convergence of organizations towards a network-based economy. As companies are more tightly interconnected and rely on business partners to develop, produce, and deliver products and services, they need to integrate resources and capabilities of the involved partners, and engage in joint implementation and utilization of new technologies that are applied and integrated into their business processes.

Blockchain based technology naturally fits in and can inherently connect partners throughout the ecosystem with the required security, enhanced trustworthy and reliability and integrity. Furthermore, blockchain is a very versatile technology and provides the means for customization, as it is not limited to any specific area of application or purpose.

Several most critical issues that enterprises should first consider are:

1. Is permissioned or permissionless blockchain best fit the business model? Most of the successful deployments are on permissioned private blockchains, as organizations really want control over who can participate, and at what capacity.
2. What types of information truly needs the inherent security and integrity mechanisms that the blockchain technology provides? Required operations are computationally very expensive and need participation of many nodes. Therefore, certain combination of data models with different level of security and integrity requirements should be established.
3. To achieve the integrity of the "distributed ledger", what level of consensus is necessary, and who can or should be trusted to provide such expensive operations in the distributed environments. This will help to select or customize the consensus mechanism in order to further improve transaction throughput.

In addition, sample business use cases in Table 1 could be applied as a way to find similar "best-fit" matches.

Technology Differentiators. Blockchain technologies will operate across the entire ecosystems, and reveal their benefits ideally on the entire business network. Therefore, the technology fitness, its offered performance and expected impact and characteristics is also key to the success of any business.

As indicated in Table 1, performance and scalability are the dominating factors that limit the applicability of a blockchain platform, especially the public chains. When analyzing business capabilities, quantitative measures such as transaction per second (TPS) for every business transaction, number of concurrent users that the system need to support, and their growth rate, etc. will have to be carefully studied. For most organizations, it may not be possible to develop their own platform or significantly enhance a chosen platform, it is necessary for architects to closely watch the most recent additions of the blockchain platforms and why they are introduced – what specific issues they tried to resolve and of course the results. For example, advances from EOS, CORDA and Solana with new data structures, innovative mechanisms for the required and "sufficient enough" consensus has gradually improved poor TPSs exhibited from the original Bitcoin and Ethereaum by 2–4 orders of magnitude, from single digits to over 60000 TPSs.

4.2 Some Key Issues to Be Further Investigated and Enhanced

Data Structures and Algorithms. From the original block structure to Merkel tree with levels of hashed information, to DAG in Corda, it is evident that significant improvements are still possible by innovating on underlying data structures that take advantage of the representational characteristics of the transactions, especially their identity information or business implications ("smart ID"[28]), business semantics [29], temporal patterns [30], etc. With matching algorithms to enforce security and integrity, they will definitely revolutionize the blockchain technology. In this regard, some self-organizing and potentially self-evolving structures, together with the help from artificial intelligence and machine learning (AI/ML), could be better fit while they could automatically do only what's necessary and sufficient.

With such innovative structures, algorithms can be further researched that take advantage of the full spectrum of analytical, stochastic and optimization, and of course AI/ML methods. Only in this way, the inefficiency of the cumbersome consensus and verification process prevailing in the current blockchain platforms can be eventually solved.

Data Models and Governance. As essentially "every company is a data company", blockchains potentially generate significant amount of new data to provide the required privacy and security, resilience and irreversibility. If bad data are offered correctly or if the data store contains false information but is offered right, they will all end up on the system.

As some high impact incidences of data loss and breach were reported that could discourage companies from transitioning to blockchains, data governance has become more critical. Poor execution of smart contracts could result in bad automated decision-making that could lead to tremendous business risks. Data privacy still remains as a challenging issue while enterprise blockchain projects need to remedy.

Performance. As discussed earlier, the performance of a blockchain could be dominated by the least "powerful" participating node in the network. So as Solana did, how to effectively enforce some minimal standards on certain node capabilities, and further classify nodes into different groups with relevant rights and privileges without sacrificing the integrity assurance, could be appealing. It is even better if we can make such decisions adaptive to the business applications and workloads.

It is also feasible to off-load some heavy processing to a secondary support chain or system, while the main blockchain is only used to record the final result of the transactions. For example, organizations always maintain some lists of "trusted" or "trust-worthy" clients, conducting transactions with those clients do not necessarily need on-time completion of all the complex hashing operations for the entire distributed ledger. Instead results from the off-loaded expensive operations only need to be reflected in the main chain, based on the "trust-worthiness" of the partners. Furthermore, such delayed mechanism could be easily designed and implemented with smart contracts!

Potentially, blockchains eliminate the requirement for intermediaries in its streamlined operations, such as transactions as well as real estate. But this is more of a business problem, as it may introduce changes to the business processes and the interaction patterns that need to be properly addressed from the strategy perspectives.

Scalability. To improve scalability, multi-layer or multi-chain systems could be introduced, as discussed before. For example, with the Lightning Network [31] of Bitcoin, a second layer to the main blockchain network is added in order to facilitate faster transactions. Plasma [32] of Ethereum has a parent-child structure, processes the transactions in the child-chain, and records the results in the parent-chain. Sharding [33] groups subsets of nodes into smaller networks or 'shards' that are responsible for the transactions specific to their shard. When offered in conjunction with the proof-of-stake consensus mechanism, such mechanisms have the potential to scale up the application.

As summarized in Table 1, private blockchain offer much better scalability, as the nodes in the network are purposely designed and enabled to process transactions in an environment of trusted parties. Therefore, some hybrid chains effectively combining public chains for certain transactions, while employing private chains for other types of transactions would provide the best combination.

In addition, in almost all known business applications, it is not required to have everyone on the eco-system to participate or contribute to establish and maintain the integrity of the distributed ledger. Therefore, policies or even smart contracts could be utilized to restrict participants.

Technically, workloads can be distributed intelligently to reduce processing needs for more "critical" (either business or technical) nodes.

Interoperability and Standardization. Another main challenge is the lack of interoperability among the large number of blockchain networks. Over 6,500 projects adopted a variety of blockchain platforms and solutions with different protocols, programming languages, consensus mechanisms, and privacy measures, while most of those blockchains work in silos and do not communicate with other peer networks. The lack of universal standards and uniformity across blockchain protocols further colluded the situation.

Various projects have initiated to address this problem. Ark uses SmartBridges [34] architecture to bridge the gap of communication between the networks and it claims to offer universal, cross-blockchain transmission and transfer with global interoperability. Cosmos [35] uses the Interblockchain Communication (IBC) protocol [36] to enable blockchain economies to operate outside silos, and transfer files between each other.

The lack of standardization also impacts interoperability and eventually lead to increased costs that make mass adoption difficult. Therefore it is vital to establish industry-wide standards and protocols to help enterprises collaborate on application development, and share blockchain solutions as well as integrate with existing systems.

While the International Organization for Standardisation is currently working on a shared global blockchain standard [37], it will be important that major industry leaders and developer communities proactively participate so that right issues, both business and technical, can be addressed.

Integration with Legacy Systems. Industries were so used to the legacy systems, especially the protocols and processes established in line with their structures. For acceptance and seamless adoption, enterprises are required to integrate them with new blockchain based solutions.

Some solutions started to emerge that enable legacy systems to connect to a blockchain backend. For example, Modex Blockchain Database [38] was designed to help organizations without much exposure in blockchains to relish the potential benefitso and remove the dangers posed by the loss of sensitive data.

Blockchain as a Service (BAAS). How can a company integrate the blockchain technology into their business without in-house expertise or experience? BaaS can offer a shortcut by packaging the smart contract technology, blockchains and network infrastructure they run on all "as services". BaaS has emerged as a popular choice because it removes much of the encumbrance of setting up a blockchain.

Some Well-Known BaaS Players Include AWS, IBM, Oracle, VMware and Alibaba. Amazon Managed Blockchain [39] is a fully managed service that allows enterprises to either join public networks or set up and manage private networks with a competitive blockchain hosting solution. For example, the Hyperledger Fabric solution's existing ordering service can be supported by Amazon QLDB technology, empowering an immutable change log and stronger data storage and security. The IBM Blockchain Platform [40] extends a wide variety of blockchain solutions to customers, from hosting and open-source development assistance to consulting and management services, and it excels in developing and managing solutions for supply chain and manufacturing. Oracle [41] offers a cloud service, an on-premises edition, and a SaaS application for supply chain management, featuring near real-time processing, validation rules and controls in smart contracts, ERP integration, exception tracking, and netting-based settlement. In addition, it is possible to adjust workload and resources to individual business model needs. VMware [42] focuses on ensuring that speed and scalability are possible while also maintaining high levels of security through fault-tolerance preservation and employs a home-grown Scalable Byzantine Fault Tolerance (SBFT), an enterprise-grade consensus engine. Alibaba's Cloud Blockchain as a Service [43] can integrate with its Video DNA service, and makes it possible for users to analyze and trade copyright data for images, video, and audio. It provides innovative end-to-end and chip encryption technologies for security, offers organization, permission, and consortium management capability, chaincode management of smart contracts, and also connection to its CloudMonitor for real-time alerts and monitoring.

Even though all those nice features are marked "as a service", they are still lack of the required standard-based "openness" and "interoperability". Setup, configuration, commitments and conformance to performance, scalability, availability, and sometimes even security and privacy still remains difficult and perplexing.

4.3 Alternatives to Blockchain Technology

Despite its promises, blockchain adoption has been very slow. Several alternatives to blockchain that provide better performance have emerged, offering organizations options to reduce costs, simplify development and reduce integration challenges while still able to enjoy some of the core benefits of blockchains.

Alternative Distributed Ledgers. A simplified distributed ledger, without the complexities involved with the current blockchain technology, is definitely an alternative for trusted decentralized applications. Several options are available, including Hashgraph, Iota Tangle and R3 Corda.

Iota and Hashgraph use Directed Acyclic Graphs (DAGs) as an alternative data structure for maintaining the ledger, while DAG approach allows an application to write data quickly, and requires permission to conduct certain operations that could slow down the transaction. The applications need to be configured to notify users when conflicts occur, and built-in rules rules to help resolve.

An Iota Tangle stores data across a DAG where each node, or vertex, represents a transaction. The network grows via transactions rather than through a compute-intensive mining process. Iota supports micropayments and transactions across IoT devices. It is mostly decentralized, but it does require a coordinator node that oversees and confirms the addition of new transactions.

Hashgraph also eliminates the need for mining to grow the ledger by utilizing its "gossip about gossip" protocol that network nodes use to share information, come to consensus (another key process in blockchain) and add new transactions to the DAG. As new data is added, an audit trail is also appended to the distributed ledger.

Centralized Ledgers. Amazon's Quantum Ledger Database simplifies the process of implementing a shared database designed for ledger-like applications that provides a cryptographically verifiable audit trail without all the overhead of a distributed ledger or blockchain. It promises the immutability and verifiability of blockchain combined with the ease and scalability of a traditional cloud service. One thing worth noting is that the blockchain could still be a better option with untrusted players.

Distributed Databases. Distributed databases offer ome combination of data replication and duplication to ensure data consistency and integrity. For example, the OrbitDB [44] open source project was built on top of a distributed filesystem that allows operation even if one node goes down, and can support the creation of a distributed, peer-to-peer databases, and it enables organizations to develop decentralized applications that run when disconnected from the internet and then sync up with other database nodes when connected. It can also allow data sharing in a way that enforces privacy and provides transparency into how data is being used.

However, for performance and usability reasons, it may still be valuable to keep and manage one highly optimized system of record in a centralized database.

Decentralized Storage. Decentralized (cloud) storage creates a resilient file storage sharing system by partitioning and encrypting data, distributing it for storage on drives on a peer-to-peer network. IPFS [45] and Storj [46] are such offerings that allow developers to store contents (data, web pages, etc.) with much-reduced bandwidth requirements, improved resilience and less impact of censorship.

Storj is another promising distributed storage technology that allows developers to encrypt files, split them into pieces and then distribute them across a global cloud network. It is directly compatible with Amazon S3 storage tools, which should make it easy for cloud developers to weave into applications without learning new tools.

5 Conclusion

It is exciting to live in this wonderful world of technologies while innovations lead to new business opportunities that in turn will present new issues calling for better solutions. This paper quickly surveyed some important issues hindering the broad enterprise adoption for the blockchains, a breakthrough that could be served as the foundation of global business transactions and exchanges, not only eliminating unnecessary intermediaries, but more importantly providing the guaranteed security and integrity of transaction information intrinsically and permanently. After some general description, we analyzed 6 representative blockchain platforms, emphasizing how each evolved to alleviate performance and scalability problems inherent in the original technology structure and algorithm stack. We then presented some quick guidelines on how organizations can select a "best-proper" platform to serve its current and future business needs.

Broad adoption of blockchain still requires significant overhaul in many critical areas, and this paper summarized some of the potential improvement opportunities. As it may take a long time before blockchain technology become mature and stable enough with the necessary transaction throughput, proper scalability and interoperability for enterprise applications, this paper finally presented some alternative technology options.

References

1. Bitcoin developer. https://developer.bitcoin.org/reference/block_chain.html. Accessed 17 Nov 2021
2. Yaga, D., Mell, P., Roby, N., Scarfone, K.: Blockchain technology overview. arXiv preprint, arXiv:1906.11078 (2019)
3. Introducing Enterprise Smart Contracts. https://azure.microsoft.com/en-us/blog/introducing-enterprise-smart-contracts/. Accessed 30 Nov 2021
4. Cao, B., Zhang, Z., Feng, D., et al.: Performance analysis and comparison of PoW, PoS and DAG based blockchains. Digit. Commun. Networks **6**(4), 480–485 (2020)
5. Zheng, Z., Xie, S., Dai, H.N., Chen, X., Wang, H.: Blockchain challenges and opportu-nities: a survey. Int. J. Web Grid Serv. **14**(4), 352–375 (2018)
6. Li, X., Jiang, P., Chen, T., Luo, X., Wen, Q.: A survey on the security of blockchain systems. Future Gener. Comput. Syst. **107**, 841–853 (2020)
7. Yakovenko, A.: Solana: a new architecture for a high performance blockchain v0. 8.13. Whitepaper (2018)
8. Monrat, A.A., Schelén, O., Andersson, K.: A survey of blockchain from the perspectives of applications, challenges, and opportunities. IEEE Access **7**, 117134–117151 (2019)
9. Sabry, S.S., Kaittan, N.M., Majeed, I.: The road to the blockchain technology: concept and types. Periodicals Eng. Nat. Sci. **7**(4), 1821–1832 (2019)
10. Kube, N.: Daniel Drescher: Blockchain Basics: A Non-Technical Introduction in 25 Steps, 1st edn. Apress, Germany (2018)
11. Dannen, C.: Introducing Ethereum and Solidity. Apress, Berkeley (2017)
12. Antonopoulos, A.M., Wood, G.: Mastering ethereum: building smart contracts and dapps. O'reilly, Media (2018)
13. Vujičić, D., Jagodić, D., Ranđić, S.: Blockchain technology, bitcoin, and Ethereum: a brief overview. In: 2018 17th International Symposium Infoteh-Jahorina (Infoteh), pp. 1–6. IEEE (2018)
14. Wood, G.: Ethereum: a secure decentralised generalised transaction ledger. Ethereum Proj. Yellow Pap. **151**(2014), 1–32 (2014)
15. Ethereum Whitepaper. https://ethereum.org/zh/whitepaper/. Accessed 04 Dec 2021
16. Transaction Execution - Ethereum Yellow Paper Walkthrough. https://www.lucassaldanha.com/transaction-execution-ethereum-yellow-paper-walkthrough-4-7/. Accessed 04 Dec 2021
17. Zheng, W., Zheng, Z., Dai, H.N., Chen, X., Zheng, P.: XBlock-EOS: extracting and exploring blockchain data from EOSIO. Inform. Process. Manage. **58**(3), 102477 (2021)
18. Ethereum VS EOS. https://www.coinsmart.com/blog/ethereum-vs-eos/. Accessed 30 Nov 2021
19. Mingxiao, D., Xiaofeng, M., Zhe, Z., Xiangwei, W., Qijun, C.: A review on consensus algorithm of blockchain. In: 2017 IEEE International Conference on Systems, Man, and Cybernetics (SMC), pp. 2567–2572. IEEE (2017)
20. Xu, G., Liu, Y., Khan, P.W.: Improvement of the DPoS consensus mechanism in blockchain based on vague sets. IEEE Trans. Ind. Inform. **16**(6), 4252–4259 (2019)

21. Zhang, S., Lee, J.H.: Analysis of the main consensus protocols of blockchain. ICT express 6(2), 93–97 (2020)
22. Yang, B., Chen, C.: Theory, Design and Application of Blockchain, 2nd edn. China Machine Press, Beijing (2020)
23. Nasir, Q., Qasse, I.A., Talib, M.A., Nassif, A.B.: Performance analysis of hyperledger fabric platforms. Secur. Commun. Networks 1, 1–14 (2018)
24. CORDA Homepage. https://www.corda.net/. Accessed 29 Nov 2021
25. Nadir, R.M.: Comparative study of permissioned blockchain solutions for enterprises. In: 2019 International Conference on Innovative Computing (ICIC), pp. 1–6. IEEE (2019)
26. Benčić, F.M., Žarko, I.P.: Distributed ledger technology: Blockchain compared to directed acyclic graph. In: 2018 IEEE 38th International Conference on Distributed Computing Systems (ICDCS), pp. 1569–1570. IEEE (2018)
27. Solana Docs Homepage. https://docs.solana.com. Accessed 31 Nov 2021
28. Cendana, D.I.: Designing a digital payment framework for HEI's using smart ID. Int. J. Comput. Theory Eng. 12(1), 1–7 (2020)
29. Norta, A.: Designing a smart-contract application layer for transacting decentralized autonomous organizations. In: International Conference on Advances in Computing and Data Sciences, pp. 595–604. Springer, Singapore (2016). https://doi.org/10.1007/978-981-10-5427-3_61
30. Tyre, M.J., Orlikowski, W.J.: Windows of opportunity: temporal patterns of techno-logical adaptation in organizations. Organ. Sci. 5(1), 98–118 (1994)
31. Poon, J., Dryja, T.: The Bitcoin Lightning Network: Scalable Off-Chain Instant Payments (2016)
32. Poon, J., Buterin, V.: Plasma: scalable autonomous smart contracts. White Pap. 472, 1–47 (2017)
33. Bez, M., Fornari, G., Vardanega, T.: The scalability challenge of Ethereum: an initial quantitative analysis. In: 2019 IEEE International Conference on Service-Oriented System Engineering (SOSE), pp. 167–176. IEEE (2019)
34. ARK Homepage. https://ark.io/. Accessed 29 Nov 2021
35. Cosmos Homepage. https://cosmos.network/. Accessed 29 Nov 2021
36. Qasse, I.A., Abu Talib, M., Nasir, Q.: Inter blockchain communication: a survey. In: Proceedings of the ArabWIC 6th Annual International Conference Research Track, pp. 1–6 (2019)
37. Gramoli, V., Staples, M.: Blockchain standard: Can we reach consensus? IEEE Commun. Stand. Mag. 2(3), 16–21 (2018)
38. Cernian, A., Vlasceanu, E., Tiganoaia, B., Iftemi, A.: Deploying block-chain technology for storing digital diplomas. In: 2021 23rd International Conference on Control Systems and Computer Science (CSCS), pp. 322–327. IEEE (2021)
39. Onik, M.M.H., Miraz, M.H.: Performance analytical comparison of blockchain-as-a-service (baas) platforms. In: International Conference for Emerging Technologies in Computing, pp. 3–18. Springer, Cham (2019). https://doi.org/10.1007/978-3-030-23943-5_1
40. IBM Blockchain Platform Homepage. https://www.ibm.com/blockchain/platform. Accessed 29 Nov 2021
41. Oracle Cloud Infrastructure Homepage. https://www.oracle.com/cloud/. Accessed 29 Nov 2021
42. Ward, B.: The Book of VMware. No Starch Press, San Francisco (2002)
43. Alibaba Cloud Homepage. https://www.alibabacloud.com/zh/product/baas. Accessed 29 Nov 2021
44. OrbitDB Homepage. https://orbitdb.org/. Accessed 29 Nov 2021
45. Benet, J.: Ipfs-content addressed, versioned, p2p file system. arXiv preprint arXiv:1407.3561 (2014)

46. Wilkinson, S., Boshevski, T., Brandoff, J., Buterin, V.: Storj a Peer-to-Peer Cloud Storage Network (2014)
47. https://www.globenewswire.com/news-release/2021/11/17/2336112/0/en/The-Blockchain-market-size-is-projected-to-grow-from-USD-4-9-billion-in-2021-to-USD-67-4-billion-by-2026-at-a-Compound-Annual-Growth-Rate-CAGR-of-68-4.html

Application Tracks

Recycling Hashes from Reversible Bitcoin Mining to Seed Pseudorandom Number Generators

Henri T. Heinonen[1]($\boxtimes$) (iD) and Alexander Semenov[2] (iD)

[1] University of Jyväskylä, Jyväskylä, Finland
`henri.t.heinonen@student.jyu.fi`
[2] University of Florida, Gainesville, FL, USA
`asemenov@ufl.edu`

Abstract. We analyzed the Bitcoin difficulty data and noticed that the difficulty has been around the level of 10^{13} for three years (H2 2018–H1 2021). Our calculation showed about 10^{28} hashes have been generated during bitcoin mining around the world for securing the addition of 703,364 blocks to the Bitcoin blockchain. We introduced a concept of Recycling Hashes in the hope to (a) jump-start bespoke silicon (customized silicon) for reversible computing, (b) open up the possibility of Bitcoin's Proof-of-Work to be less energy-consuming in the future, (c) provide scientific value or new services, in the form of entropy pool or random numbers, to Internet users while still achieving the security level of Bitcoin of today, (d) decrease the old mining hardware e-waste by using them to recycle hashes to the entropy pool, and (e) solve the problem of low mining rewards. We found that the bit rates of the current irreversible bitcoin miners are millions of times as high as the existing Internet connections, so it would be difficult to send all the hashes generated in real-time via the Internet. Even if only 0.000000355% of the hashes can be recycled, it would still mean that $355 \cdot 10^{18}$ hashes (355 EH) would have been recycled since the beginning of Bitcoin. Storing all the hashes, so far, would need storage of $2.560 \cdot 10^{30}$ bits, and it is not currently possible to keep all of them. Our simulation of 10,000 bitcoin hashes showed that the occurrences of zeros and ones in bitcoin hashes are almost 50% and 50%, so it is an encouraging finding for seeding the Pseudorandom Number Generators. We also proposed a second coin for the Bitcoin blockchain, an inflationary coin with a different currency unit (BTCi), to motivate the entropy providers to keep the old mining hardware online. The proposed second coin might keep Bitcoin's security model safe in the future when the deflationary bitcoin (BTC or BTCd) block reward is becoming too low.

Keywords: Reversible computing · Bitcoin mining · Random number generation

Supported by Liikesivistysrahasto.

K. Lee and L.-J. Zhang (Eds.): ICBC 2021, LNCS 12991, pp. 103–117, 2022.
https://doi.org/10.1007/978-3-030-96527-3_7

1   Introduction

In this paper, "Bitcoin" (with uppercase B) is the Bitcoin protocol and the Bitcoin network and "bitcoin" (with lowercase b) is the bitcoin money. Bitcoin was introduced in 2008 by Satoshi Nakamoto [3] and the Bitcoin blockchain was started in 2009. Bitcoin mining has been a controversial topic since the mid-2010s. In 2009 and the early 2010s, CPUs (Central Processing Units) were used for bitcoin mining resembling grid computing projects like those utilizing the BOINC (Berkeley Open Infrastructure for Network Computing) platform. In the mid-2010s, bitcoin mining by CPUs was not profitable anymore because there was already bitcoin mining software using the computer graphics card's GPU (Graphics Processing Unit). The next stage in bitcoin mining evolution was the introduction of FPGA (Field-Programmable Gate Array) chips that were even faster at producing SHA256d (double SHA256) (SHA-2 means Secure Hash Algorithm 2) hashes than GPUs. This stage was even shorter than the GPU bitcoin mining stage because some bespoke silicon projects successfully developed and produced ASICs (Application Specific Integrated Circuits) for bitcoin mining.

SHA256d ASICs can only be used to calculate SHA256d hashes; Scrypt ASICs, used for mining litecoin (LTC), can only be used to calculate Scrypt hashes. For comparison, FPGAs can be programmed to do different calculations, and modern GPUs can also be used flexibly. ASICs are not for general computing, but they are swift. The problem with bitcoin ASIC mining is that the chips are still using lots of energy for the calculations. Another problem is that bitcoin ASIC mining devices are "getting old" very fast. It is not profitable to keep old mining hardware online because newer mining hardware will produce hashes at a faster rate and produce more bitcoin income for the hardware owner. Suppose the cost of bitcoin mining is higher than the bitcoin mining revenue. In that case, the only solution is to sell the mining hardware to someone living in an area where electricity is cheaper. Eventually, it is not profitable to use the old hardware for mining anywhere on the planet. The old mining hardware has become "e-waste".

One alternative solution is to use the old hardware to mine some altcoins with the same hash function (SHA256d) Bitcoin is using. One example is namecoin (NMC) that can be mined either alone or merge mined together with bitcoin, but mining altcoins is still not consistently profitable even in the case of merge mining. Merge mining means mining two or more similar kinds of cryptocurrencies simultaneously without sacrificing overall mining performance.

1.1   Bitcoin Mining

Bitcoin mining is a type of lottery game where one competes against other bitcoin miners. The more mining power (the higher the hash rate) one has, the better is the chance to win in this competition. The winner will get permission to add a new block with bitcoin transactions onto the Bitcoin blockchain. The winner will also get a reward that consists of a block reward of several bitcoin (BTC).

The winner will also get the transaction fees (also paid in BTC) added by the users whose transactions were included in the new block.

Difficulty is a measure of how difficult it is to find a hash below a given target. The Bitcoin network has a global block difficulty that is recalculated every 2016 blocks. Because the desired rate of Bitcoin blocks is ten minutes, it would take two weeks to mine 2016 blocks. If it takes less than two weeks for 2016 new blocks, the difficulty will go up; if it takes more than two weeks for 2016 new blocks, the difficulty will go down [6].

Bitcoin blocks are generally around 1 MB in size in 2021. Blocks include transaction data and also headers that contain metadata. There are 80 bytes or 640 bits in the header of a Bitcoin block. The output of the SHA256 (and SHA256d) function is a 256-bit number. This means that the chip to calculate Bitcoin's SHA256d hash function has 640 input wires and 256 output wires.

Mining bitcoin needs lots of electricity. Stoll et al. estimate "the annual electricity consumption of Bitcoin" in November 2018 to be 45.8 TWh and the annual carbon emissions range from 22.0 to 22.9 $MtCO_2$ [36]. For comparison, the use of electricity in Finland totalled 86.1 TWh in 2019 [15], the total energy consumption in Finland in 2019 was 1362 PJ or 378 TWh [9], and the total emissions of carbon dioxide (CO2 eq.) in Finland in 2020 was 48.3 million tonnes [5]. According to the Galaxy Digital Mining report from May 2021 [12], Bitcoin consumed 113.89 TWh of electricity annually, the gold industry used about 240.61 TWh of energy annually, and the banking industry consumed 263.72 TWh of energy annually. They compare Bitcoin's electricity usage to the global annual energy supply (1,458.2 times that of the Bitcoin network), the global annual electricity generation (234.7 times that of the Bitcoin network), the amount of electricity lost in transmission and distribution each year (19.4 times that of the Bitcoin network), and the energy footprint of "always-on" devices in American households (12.1 times that of the Bitcoin network). It is also useful to compare the bitcoin mining electricity usage to the electricity and energy usages of other IT industries' activities. PC gaming used about 75 TWh of electricity in 2012 according to Mills et al. [34] Facebook's global electricity consumption was 5.14 TWh in 2019 according to Alves [8]. The energy consumption of Google (Alphabet) was 12.7 TWh in 2019, according to Jaganmohan [1]. According to Alden [4], Bitcoin's energy usage is not a problem because the mining uses less than 0.1% of global energy and because a sizable portion of the energy used for mining would be otherwise stranded and wasted.

Bitcoin mining is based on a "Proof-of-Work" (PoW) mechanism, the idea that a miner needs to spend a sufficient amount of work to receive the compensation. In Bitcoin, it is implemented based on the principle that it is easy to validate the correctness of a cryptographic SHA256d hash given the input and the resulting hash, but it is very hard (or impossible) to find the input for the hash function from the particular output. Generally, to find an input value for a hash function given its output, one should brute force possible inputs. During the bitcoin mining process, miners compete in finding the *nonce*, a value that is along with details of new transactions and a link to the previous block, a part of the input to the SHA256d functions. The goal is to find such a nonce that the number of leading zeros in the output would be greater than a certain threshold, set by the difficulty. The more leading zeros should be at the beginning of the output, the harder it is to find a suitable *nonce* value. By finding the nonce, new transactions are added into the blockchain, and modifications of the transactions in this block would require finding another nonce in the current and potential subsequent blocks. Thus, the bitcoin mining process consists of repeated calculations of SHA256d hashes and checking if they suit the difficulty constraint.

1.2 Reversible Computing

Almost all of the computing in the world today (including bitcoin mining) is irreversible. From the chip's output, the final state $f(x)$, it is difficult or impossible to figure out the intermediate states and the initial state x. Reversible computing is a computational model where the computational process can be reversed in time, i.e., its previous states can be reconstructed from its subsequent states. For example, specific inputs of logical exclusive OR (XOR) cannot be obtained from its output, as multiple different inputs may correspond to the output; however, the input of NOT operation can be determined based on its output. According to Frank [14], reversible computing refers to computing in a way that preserves signal energies and reuses them over multiple digital operations. Reversible computing focuses on achieving far greater energy efficiency and practical performance for all digital computing, rather than quantum speedups on relatively few specialized applications.

In 1961 Rolf Landauer [31] noticed that logically irreversible gate will dissipate heat to its environment according to the equation

$$E = k_{\mathrm{B}}T\ln(2). \tag{1}$$

In Eq. (1), k_{B} is the Boltzmann constant, T is the temperature of the environment in kelvins, and $\ln(2)$ is the natural logarithm of 2.

With reversible computing, it would be possible to *uncompute* the final state $f(x)$ and go back all the way to the initial state x. By not wasting any information, reversible computing could be highly energy-efficient. Making computing reversible could reduce the excess generation of waste heat. Quantum computing is closely related to reversible computing. Frank et al. [24] note that (a) Landauer's Principle sets a strict lower bound on entropy generation in traditional non-reversible architectures for deterministic computing machines; and (b) reversible computing can potentially circumvent the Landauer limit with the potential of allowing the efficiency of future digital computing to improve indefinitely.

1.3 Generating Pseudorandom Numbers

Random numbers in classical computing systems are generally pseudorandom numbers because it is impossible to get truly random numbers from computers considered deterministic. The big difference is quantum computing that makes true random number generation possible. For example, Heinonen [25] shows a simple example of how to generate a quantum program that generates true random numbers.

Here we consider classical computing systems, so we concentrate on the PRNGs (Pseudorandom Number Generators). There are PRNGs such as Blum Blum Shub [21], Yarrow [29], and Fortuna [22]. Fortuna is a modern and cryptographically secure PRNG. It is a family of secure PRNGs, and they consist of the following parts: (a) the generator, which once seeded will produce pseudo-random data; (b) the entropy accumulator, which collects random data from various sources and reseeds the generator when possible; (c) the seed file, which stores entropy for the computer to start generating random numbers after rebooting.

1.4   Literature Review

We know from Stoll et al. [36] that bitcoin mining uses lots of energy and has a considerable carbon footprint. de Vries et al. [40] found that bitcoin mining generates lots of hardware waste or *e-waste*: 30.7 metric kilotons annually as of May 2021. de Vries [39] estimated mining equipment to become obsolete in roughly 1.5 years.

It is exciting that reversible computing is not a new invention, but it is still not used as of writing this article. Bennett [19] found already in 1973 that every classical computation can be turned into reversible form. Toffoli [38] invented a universal reversible logic gate in 1980. According to Frank [23], reversible computing could be from 1000 to 100,000 as cost-effective as irreversible computing in the 2050s. The IBM Q Experience quantum computing documentation has an excellent introduction to reversible computing [7].

We also know various consensus methods that have the potential to replace the energy-consuming Proof-of-Work consensus methods. For example, Ethereum developers are trying to replace Ethereum's Proof-of-Work with Proof-of-Stake (PoS). We know projects like Gridcoin [10], and Primecoin [30] do valuable science while securing the blockchains with their consensus methods. Bizzaro et al. [20] introduce Proof-of-Evolution (PoE) that keeps the security features of Proof-of-Work, and uses part of the mining computations for the execution of genetic algorithms (GAs). Miller et al. [33] try to repurpose Bitcoin work for data preservation. Manthey et al. [32] try to replace brute force mining algorithm with solving Boolean satisfiability problem (SAT).

Bitcoin's transaction fees are too low to motivate bitcoin miners, according to Kaşkaloğlu [28] and Cussen [17]. According to Alden [4], the Bitcoin network continues to be more energy-efficient each year due to the declining block rewards.

According to Taylor [37], bitcoin ASIC mining is proof that bespoke silicon (customized silicon) can be developed in small volumes. These devices outperform general-purpose SoCs developed by major multi-billion dollar companies.

Ferguson et al. [22] note that backups and virtual machines cause problems when reseeding PRNGs. The problem is that PRNG that loads the seed file from backups will be reseeded from the very same seed file. Until the accumulator has collected enough entropy, the PRNG will produce the same output after two reboots. They claim that there is no direct defense against this kind of attack.

Wang et al. [41] present RandChain, a decentralized random beacon protocol designed to provide continuous randomness at regular intervals.

According to the literature research, we do not have solid answers to the following questions.

1. How to secure the Bitcoin blockchain without a huge carbon footprint and lots of mining hardware e-waste? There are consensus methods like Proof-of-Stake, but they are not ready to replace Proof-of-Work yet.
2. The information in reversible computing needs to be stored somewhere. Where and how will it be stored? Will it be stored locally or globally?
3. There seems to be not enough incentive to build reversible computers. How to stimulate the development of reversible computing hardware and software?
4. When there is not enough entropy available, how to seed PRNGs without using the same seed file during the computer startup process?
5. People who do not use bitcoin tend to state that bitcoin is not valuable. How to make Bitcoin more valuable and justified even for those who do not want to use the bitcoin cryptocurrency itself? One method to provide new value to the system is to solve science problems while securing the blockchain. There are inventions like Proof-of-Evolution, Primecoin, and Permacoin, but Bitcoin is not using their methods.

Research Question. Our research question is: How to change bitcoin mining to use potentially less energy and do something valuable besides securing the Bitcoin blockchain?

1.5 Recycling Hashes from Reversible Bitcoin Mining to Seed Pseudorandom Number Generators

We try to answer our Research Question by introducing Recycling Hashes from Reversible Bitcoin Mining to Seed Pseudorandom Number Generators. Using reversible computing for bitcoin mining has been discussed on the Bitcoin Forum [13]. Seeding PRNGs with random data is a familiar concept, and methods like LavaRand use digitalized fresh images of lava lamps to seed PRNGs.

What kind of a chip would mine bitcoin using reversible computing? The exact number of input and output wires for the R-SHA256d chip is unknown because reversible computing architectures are still in the early stages. There will probably be more input and, especially, output wires for the reversible SHA256d chip than for the irreversible SHA256d chip.

Is not it impossible to reverse a secure hash function? Reversible computing is not breaking the secure hash functions (including SHA256). It will only echo the input wires x to output wires x, calculate the final state $f(x)$ and generate some garbage data, intermediate states $g(x)$, from clean scratch memory $000\ldots$ (L zeros). All it does is mapping x, 0^L to x, $g(x)$, and $f(x)$. It is impossible to use the output from SHA256 (or SHA256d) in R-SHA256 (or R-SHA256d) to figure out the input. The output of SHA256 (and SHA256d) is missing the x and $g(x)$ information that would be needed for going back to the initial state x.

The idea of using reversible bitcoin mining to generate random numbers did not come from reversible computing but from the need to find some usage of the billions of hashes generated during the mining process. There is the famous LavaRand method [35] to generate random numbers by taking digital pictures of lava lamps, converting the information to binary numbers, applying a cryptographic hash function, obtaining seed from the hash function, and feeding that seed to the PRNG. Our idea was to take the otherwise wasted hashes of bitcoin mining and feed them to the Bitcoin network users to seed their PRNGs. This idea was getting more justified in reversible computing. Erasing information means generating waste heat. The erasing of information can be avoided if the information is copied to *a clean auxiliary register* before uncomputing the solution $f(x)$ [7].

What if most or at least some of the otherwise wasted hashes of mining could be recycled somehow? Could they be stored onto the blockchain or sent securely to the Bitcoin network users so they can seed their PRNGs? The peer-to-peer network of Bitcoin (or the blockchain itself) could act as the auxiliary register to record the information before it gets uncomputed (and erased). The Fortuna PRNG has a problem with the seed files when using virtual machines or backups because the same seed file will be used. Our solution of using fresh seeds from the blockchain network's entropy pool could solve this problem. It will need an Internet connection to get fresh seeds from the blockchain network.

2   Methods

Bitcoin difficulty is a measure of the mining power available securing the Bitcoin blockchain. The Bitcoin difficulty changes every 2016 blocks (two weeks if there are 10 min between each block) to correspond to the changes in total hash rate. We got the Bitcoin difficulty data from Blockchain.com website [11] and a bitcoin miner's technical specs from the producer's website [2].

The Bitcoin network's total hash rate measures the number of hashes the miners worldwide are generating when mining bitcoin in one second. We got the Bitcoin network's total hash rate data from the Blockchain.com website [16].

We simulated mining Bitcoin's Genesis block with Python code to generate 10,000 hashes until the mining ended with finding the correct hash. We stored the hashes as binary numbers into a file sample.bin. The file contained 2,560,000 binary numbers (zeros and ones). We run the Fourmilab's Pseudorandom Number Sequence Test Program, ent, with the following command:

```
ent -c sample.bin > sample.bak
```

Table 1. Table showing the bit rate of the miner divided by the upload speed of the Internet connection. The slower speeds (Gbit/s) are the Internet upload speeds and the faster speeds (Pbit/s) are the bit rates of the miners.

	2.816 Pbit/s	28.160 Pbit/s	281.600 Pbit/s
0.1 Gbit/s	281,600,000	2,816,000,000	28,160,000,000
1.0 Gbit/s	28,160,000	*281,600,000*	2,816,000,000
10 Gbit/s	2,816,000	28,160,000	281,600,000

3   Results

In this section we introduce the results: difficulty and hash rate of Bitcoin over time, the total number of hashes generated in bitcoin mining, and our small pseudorandom number sequence test to check the occurrences of ones and zeros in the set of 10,000 hashes, the entropy of the data set and some other statistics generated by the ent program.

3.1   Difficulty, Hash Rate, and Total Number of Hashes

We plotted the Bitcoin difficulty in function of time in Fig. 1 and the Bitcoin network's total hash rate in function of time in Fig. 2. We calculated the integral of the Bitcoin network's total hash rate (hashes per second) data, $H(t)$, over the time period of early 2009 to this date by using Python SciPy's trapezoid function and got the result of

$$\int_{t=T(\text{2009-01-02 23:00:00})}^{T(\text{2021-09-30 00:00:00})} H(t)\,\mathrm{d}t = 1.059466790224828 \cdot 10^{28} \text{ hashes} \approx 10^{28} \text{ hashes.}$$

(2)

The number of hashes in Eq. (2) means that storing all of them would need storage of $2.560 \cdot 10^{30}$ bits.

According to [2] Antminer S19 Pro has a hash rate of 110 TH/s, so it can generate $110 \cdot 10^{12}$ SHA256d hashes per second. One SHA256d hash has 256 bits, so the bit rate of the miner is $28.16 \cdot 10^{15}$ bit/s or 28.160 Pbit/s. We calculated various different upload speeds and bitcoin miner's bit rates in Table 1.

3.2   Pseudorandom Number Sequence Test

We used the program called *ent* to test our sequence of 10,000 hashes stored in a file that contained 2,560,000 zeros and ones.

Table 2 shows the fractions of ones and zeros in our file with 10,000 simulated bitcoin hashes. The test results from the ent program were stored in a file sample.bak.

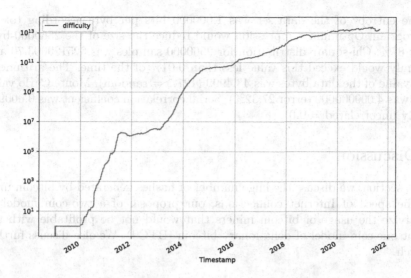

Fig. 1. The difficulty of Bitcoin during the years.

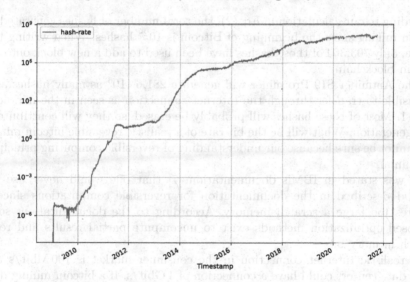

Fig. 2. The total hash rate (H/s) of Bitcoin network during the years.

Table 2. Table showing the ASCII values of the characters, their occurrences and fractions of the whole data set.

ASCII value	Character	Occurrences	Fraction
48	0	1280136	0.500053
49	1	1279864	0.499947
Total		2560000	1.000000

The entropy of the data set was 1.000000 bits per byte according to the ent program. Optimum compression would reduce the size of the 2560000-byte file by 87%. Chi-square distribution for 2560000 samples was 325120003.70 and randomly would exceed this value less than 0.01% of the time. The arithmetic mean value of the data bytes was 48.4999 (127.5 = random). Monte Carlo value for Pi was 4.000000000 (error 27.32%). Serial correlation coefficient was 0.000944 (totally uncorrelated = 0.0).

4   Discussion

In this section, we discuss the huge number of hashes generated by bitcoin mining, the speed of Internet connections, our proposal of a two-coin model to incentivize the usage of bitcoin miners that would not be profitable with the current one-coin model of deflationary bitcoin (BTCd). We also discuss further research.

4.1   The Number of Hashes and the Speed of Internet Connections

According to our calculation in Eq. (2), the total number of hashes generated by bitcoin mining since the beginning of Bitcoin is 10^{28} hashes. When writing this article, only 703,364 of those hashes have been used to add a new block onto the Bitcoin blockchain.

The Antminer S19 Pro miner will generate $281.6 \cdot 10^6$ as many hashes as it is possible to transfer through the Internet connection as seen in the middle of Table 1. Most of these hashes will probably be erased, so they will contribute to heat generation. What will be the bit rate of a realistic reversible bitcoin miner? We cannot be sure because our understanding of reversible computing principles is minimal.

It was stated in IBM's documentation [7] that one would never use the method described in the documentation for reversible computations since it requires too large a scratch memory. According to the documentation, some proposed optimization methods exist to uncompute partial results and reuse scratch memory bits.

A realistic Internet connection in the consumer market is 100 Mbit/s and small data centers could have a connection of 1 Gbit/s. If a bitcoin mining data center has ten Antminer S19 Pro miners and a 1 Gbit/s Internet connection, then the bit rate of the miners is 2,816,000,000 times the speed of the Internet connection. This would mean that

$$\frac{281,600,000\,\text{Gbit/s} - 1\,\text{Gbit/s}}{281,600,000\,\text{Gbit/s}} \cdot 100\% = 99.9999996448863636\ldots\%$$

of the generated hashes will be destroyed and only $0.0000003551136\ldots\%$ of the generated hashes will be recycled. Even if only 0.000000355% of the hashes can be recycled, it would still mean that $0.0000000355 \cdot 10^{28} = 355 \cdot 10^{18}$ hashes (355 EH) would have been recycled since the beginning of Bitcoin!

Storing all the hashes would mean storing $2.560 \cdot 10^{30}$ bits, but it is not feasible at the moment. According to Barnett [18], in 2016, the whole Internet traffic generated one zettabyte or about $8 \cdot 10^{21}$ bits of information.

Our simulation of 10,000 hashes showed, in Table 2, that the occurrences of zeros and ones in bitcoin hashes are almost 50% and 50%, so it is probably an encouraging finding for seeding the PRNGs.

4.2 Two-Coin Model

In this work, we proposed a second coin for the Bitcoin blockchain, an inflationary coin with a different currency unit (BTCi), to motivate the entropy providers to keep the old mining hardware online. The second coin might keep Bitcoin's security model safe in the future when the deflationary bitcoin (BTC or XBT or BTCd) block reward is becoming too low. The deflationary bitcoin coin (BTCd) comes with the famous cap of 21 million coins in total, but the inflationary bitcoin coin (BTCi) does not necessarily have any cap at all.

Having inflationary coins in the same blockchain ecosystem could also provide a solution to the problem of coin hoarding, holding, or "hodling". Inflationary coins would motivate (inflationary) bitcoin users to spend their money because inflation would eventually decrease the second coin's monetary value.

There are at least two different reasons why inflationary coin would solve the problem of "low mining rewards": (a) The inflationary bitcoin coin, which is given as a reward to the entropy providers (especially to the old mining hardware users), would probably motivate to keep on mining because the BTCi coin would have a monetary value even if it was not as expensive as the BTCd coin; and (b) the inflationary coin would probably raise the number of transactions in a block because the inflationary nature of BTCi coin would make people to use it more frequently than they use the deflationary BTCd coin. The more transactions are included in a block, the higher are the total transaction fees per block.

4.3 Further Research

Further research would include using real bitcoin miners to generate seeds for PRNGs. It would be interesting to know if this could become a practical way to generate good quality random numbers in the future.

There needs to be more research on reversible computing principles. It would be interesting to know if quantum computing groups could also do more research on reversible (classical) computing because reversible computing and quantum computing are closely related.

There must also be more research on many-coin cryptoeconomies. How would the bitcoin economy change if a hard fork introduces a second coin into the blockchain, for example, the inflationary BTCi coin? In the Ethereum ecosystem, the ether coin (ETH) and thousands of smart contract tokens are mainly running without any significant issues. Heinonen et al. [27] found some differences in behaviour between the ERC-20 (ERC means Ethereum Request for

Comments) tokens and stockmarket. Heinonen [26] introduced the two-money cryptoeconomy of money and antimoney.

5   Conclusion

Our research question was: How to change bitcoin mining to use potentially less energy and do something valuable besides securing the Bitcoin blockchain?

Assuming the difficulty of Bitcoin will stay around 10^{13}, we found out that even with a reversible bitcoin miner, lots of heat will probably be generated because most of the generated hashes (information) will be erased in a way or another. The good side is that recycling hashes from bitcoin mining to PRNGs provides new value to the Bitcoin network. This entropy pool service could be available even for those who do not do bitcoin mining nor use bitcoin cryptocurrency nor the Bitcoin blockchain at all.

There may be breakthroughs in Internet connection speeds, mass storage, and reversible computing principles to overcome these issues. Still, it is challenging not to waste any energy during blockchain operations. Even if there are no breakthroughs in these technologies, our finding that

$$\text{hashes accepted (current block height)} \lll \text{hashes potentially recycled}$$
$$\lll \text{hashes generated}$$

still motivates to pursue hash recycling.

Our proposal could be a solution for the problem of bitcoin mining hardware e-waste. One could use one's old (reversible/irreversible) ASIC bitcoin miner to generate hashes for the Bitcoin entropy pool even though the miner device is too old to create profitable deflationary bitcoin coins (BTCd) anymore. The incentive for mining with old hardware could come from the inflationary bitcoin coins (BTCi).

We hope that our concept of Recycling Hashes from Reversible Bitcoin Mining to Seed Pseudorandom Number Generators could:

1. Jump-start bespoke silicon for reversible computing.
2. Open up the possibility of Bitcoin's Proof-of-Work to be less energy-consuming in the future.
3. Provide scientific value or new services, in the form of entropy pool or random numbers, to Internet users while still achieving the security level of Bitcoin of today.
4. Decrease the old mining hardware e-waste by using them to recycle hashes to the entropy pool.
5. Solve the problem of low mining rewards.

Acknowledgements. We thank Professor Pekka Neittaanmäki and Professor Timo Hämäläinen for discussions and feedback. Henri thanks Liikesivistysrahasto (200092) for support.

References

1. Alphabet (google): energy consumption 2019 — statista. https://web.archive.org/web/20211029095928/www.statista.com/statistics/788540/energy-consumption-of-google/. Accessed 08 Nov 2021
2. Antminer s19 pro - the future of mining. https://web.archive.org/web/20210906102302/shop.bitmain.com/release/AntminerS19Pro/overview. Accessed 06 Sep 2021
3. Bitcoin: A peer-to-peer electronic cash system. https://web.archive.org/web/20211103223918/bitcoin.org/bitcoin.pdf. Accessed 04 Nov 2021
4. Bitcoin's energy usage isn't a problem. here's why. https://web.archive.org/web/20211103232331/www.lynalden.com/bitcoin-energy/. Accessed 08 Nov 2021
5. Carbon dioxide emissions - motiva. https://web.archive.org/web/20201030003703/www.motiva.fi/en/solutions/energy_use_in_finland/carbon_dioxide_emissions. Accessed 26 Oct 2021
6. Difficulty - bitcoin wiki. https://web.archive.org/web/20210813113701/en.bitcoin.it/wiki/Difficulty. Accessed 29 Sep 2021
7. Docs and resources - IBM quantum experience - shor's algorithm. https://web.archive.org/web/20201101072900/quantum-computing.ibm.com/docs/iqx/guide/shors-algorithm. Accessed 06 Sep 2021
8. Facebook electricity usage globally 2019 — statista. https://web.archive.org/web/20210818230043/www.statista.com/statistics/580087/energy-use-of-facebook/. Accessed 08 Nov 2021
9. Final consumption of energy - motiva. https://web.archive.org/web/20211026171442/www.motiva.fi/en/solutions/energy_use_in_finland/final_consumption_of_energy. Accessed 26 Oct 2021
10. Gridcoin white paper - the computation power of a blockchain driving science and data analysis. https://web.archive.org/web/20210815003224/gridcoin.us/assets/docs/whitepaper.pdf. Accessed 04 Nov 2021
11. Network difficulty - a relative measure of how difficult it is to mine a new block for the blockchain. https://www.blockchain.com/charts/difficulty. Accessed 03 Sep 2021
12. On bitcoin's energy consumption: A quantitative approach to a subjective question. https://web.archive.org/web/20211108150128/docsend.com/view/adwmdeeyfvqwecj2. Accessed 08 Nov 2021
13. Re: Theoretical minimum # of logic operations to perform double iterated sha256? https://web.archive.org/web/20210906102310/bitcointalk.org/index.php?topic=1029536.msg11145144. Accessed 06 Sep 2021
14. Reversible computing: The only future for general digital computing. https://web.archive.org/web/20210401031527/cfwebprod.sandia.gov/cfdocs/CompResearch/docs/LPS21-talk-v5.pdf. Accessed 01 Oct 2021
15. Statistics Finland - energy supply and consumption. https://web.archive.org/web/20210414035155/www.stat.fi/til/ehk/2019/ehk_2019_2020-12-21_tie_001_en.html. Accessed 08 Nov 2021
16. Total hash rate (th/s) - the estimated number of terahashes per second the bitcoin network is performing in the last 24 hours. https://www.blockchain.com/charts/hash-rate. Accessed 03 Oct 2021
17. Turning off bitcoin's inflation funded security model - wishful thinking? https://web.archive.org/web/20211012055718/www.onionfutures.com/turning-off-bitcoins-inflation. Accessed 26 Oct 2021

18. The zettabyte era officially begins (how much is that?). https://web.archive.org/web/20210813122554/blogs.cisco.com/sp/the-zettabyte-era-officially-begins-how-much-is-that. Accessed 04 Oct 2021
19. Bennett, C.H.: Logical reversibility of computation. IBM J. Res. Dev. 17(6), 525–532 (1973). https://doi.org/10.1147/rd.176.0525
20. Bizzaro, F., Conti, M., Pini, M.S.: Proof of evolution: leveraging blockchain mining for a cooperative execution of genetic algorithms. In: 2020 IEEE International Conference on Blockchain (Blockchain), pp. 450–455. IEEE (2020)
21. Blum, L., Blum, M., Shub, M.: A simple unpredictable pseudo-random number generator. SIAM J. Comput. 15(2), 364–383 (1986)
22. Ferguson, N., Schneier, B., Kohno, T.: Cryptography Engineering: Design Principles and Practical Applications. Wiley, Hoboken (2011)
23. Frank, M.P.: Nanocomputer Systems Engineering. CRC Press, Boca Raton (2006)
24. Frank, M.P., Shukla, K.: Quantum foundations of classical reversible computing. Entropy 23(6), 701 (2021)
25. Heinonen, H.: Katsaus kvanttilaskentateknologiaan ja sen sovelluksiin. Informaatioteknologian tiedekunnan julkaisuja 88/2021, 1–79 (2021). https://jyx.jyu.fi/handle/123456789/74322
26. Heinonen, H.T.: On creation of a stablecoin based on the Morini's scheme of Inv&Sav wallets and antimoney. Accepted to IEEE Workshop on Blockchain Security, Application, and Performance (BSAP 2021) (2021)
27. Heinonen, H.T., Semenov, A., Boginski, V.: Collective behavior of price changes of ERC-20 tokens. In: Chellappan, S., Choo, K.-K.R., Phan, N.H. (eds.) CSoNet 2020. LNCS, vol. 12575, pp. 487–498. Springer, Cham (2020). https://doi.org/10.1007/978-3-030-66046-8_40
28. Kaskaloglu, K.: Near zero bitcoin transaction fees cannot last forever (2014)
29. Kelsey, J., Schneier, B., Ferguson, N.: Yarrow-160: notes on the design and analysis of the yarrow cryptographic pseudorandom number generator. In: Heys, H., Adams, C. (eds.) SAC 1999. LNCS, vol. 1758, pp. 13–33. Springer, Heidelberg (2000). https://doi.org/10.1007/3-540-46513-8_2
30. King, S.: Primecoin: Cryptocurrency with prime number proof-of-work (2013). July 7th 1(6)
31. Landauer, R.: Irreversibility and heat generation in the computing process. IBM J. Res. Dev. 5(3), 183–191 (1961)
32. Manthey, N., Heusser, J.: Satcoin-bitcoin mining via sat. In: SAT COMPETITION 2018, p. 67 (2018)
33. Miller, A., Juels, A., Shi, E., Parno, B., Katz, J.: Permacoin: repurposing bitcoin work for data preservation. In: 2014 IEEE Symposium on Security and Privacy, pp. 475–490. IEEE (2014)
34. Mills, N., Mills, E.: Taming the energy use of gaming computers. Energ. Effi. 9(2), 321–338 (2015). https://doi.org/10.1007/s12053-015-9371-1
35. Noll, L.C., Mende, R.G., Sisodiya, S.: Method for seeding a pseudo-random number generator with a cryptographic hash of a digitization of a chaotic system. US Patent 5,732,138, 24 March 1998
36. Stoll, C., Klaaßen, L., Gallersdörfer, U.: The carbon footprint of bitcoin. Joule 3(7), 1647–1661 (2019)
37. Taylor, M.B.: Bitcoin and the age of bespoke silicon. In: 2013 International Conference on Compilers, Architecture and Synthesis for Embedded Systems (CASES), pp. 1–10. IEEE (2013)

38. Toffoli, T.: Reversible computing. In: de Bakker, J., van Leeuwen, J. (eds.) ICALP 1980. LNCS, vol. 85, pp. 632–644. Springer, Heidelberg (1980). https://doi.org/10.1007/3-540-10003-2_104

39. de Vries, A.: Renewable energy will not solve bitcoin's sustainability problem. Joule **3**(4), 893–898 (2019)

40. de Vries, A., Stoll, C.: Bitcoin's growing e-waste problem. Resour. Conserv. Recycl. **175**, 105901 (2021)

41. Wang, G., Nixon, M.: Randchain: practical scalable decentralized randomness attested by blockchain. In: 2020 IEEE International Conference on Blockchain (Blockchain), pp. 442–449. IEEE (2020)

Preserving Privacy in Private Blockchain Networks

Prabhakaran Ariappampalayam Krishnamoorthi[✉], Saad Shahid, and Oisín Boydell

CeADAR - Ireland's Centre for Applied AI, School of Computer Science, University College Dublin, Dublin, Ireland
prabhakaran.ak@ucd.ie

Abstract. In contrast to public blockchains, private and permissioned blockchains enable specific organizations to come together and maintain a distributed and decentralized ledger to which only those specific participants have access. These private blockchains are favoured in scenarios where there is a particular emphasis on data privacy, such as in the exchange of electronic health records (EHRs) for example. However, managing *internal* data privacy within private blockchain platforms, i.e. which participants can see which data, is not a trivial task. Existing solutions such as private data collections, attribute based encryption and multi-party computation all have their limitations. In this paper, we propose an alternative approach based on asymmetric cryptography and we show how this can alleviate many of the current shortcomings.

1 Introduction

Blockchains are distributed and fault-tolerant networks that can be either public or private. The difference between them being who is allowed to participate in the network and in the consensus protocol that ensures synchronization and immutability of transactions. Public blockchains, as the name suggests, are open to anyone to participate. Their transactions are visible to all and any participant can take part in the consensus process. Bitcoin [1] and Ethereum [2] are examples of public blockchains.

Private and permissioned blockchains on the other hand are restricted to specific authorized or verified participants. For example, a group of organizations can come together and maintain a distributed and decentralized ledger between them which only they can access, and these are generally favoured for enterprise deployments as well as use cases where data privacy is of particular concern. Hyperledger Fabric [3] and R3 Corda [4] are well-known examples of such private or permissioned blockchain frameworks.

A relevant use case for private and permissioned blockchains which we use throughout our work for illustrative purposes is the exchange of private health data through EHR (Electronic Health Records) [5–7]. Figure 1 shows an example EHR with various stakeholders such as hospitals, general practitioners, health

© Springer Nature Switzerland AG 2022
K. Lee and L.-J. Zhang (Eds.): ICBC 2021, LNCS 12991, pp. 118–128, 2022.
https://doi.org/10.1007/978-3-030-96527-3_8

insurance companies, pharmacies and of course the patient themselves who require controlled access to specific fields of the data. The security and privacy of such data is critical, with specific laws and regulations governing the privacy of health data within most jurisdictions being common.

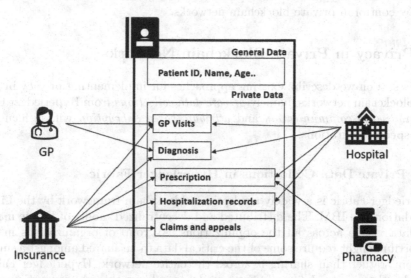

Fig. 1. An example Electronic Health Record (EHR) with various stakeholders requiring controlled access to specific fields of the data

Private blockchains handle data as a state entity. A state in blockchain is a defined digital representation of an asset. There can be different kinds of states for a blockchain application, for example the maintenance of an EHR can include multiple states such as the patient's personal record, GP visits, hospitalization records, claim reports and prescriptions etc. All these state entities are created, verified and stored with the help of transactions.

When it comes to the transaction model of private blockchain frameworks, there are two major categories. Peer-to-peer messaging is where the state entity is visible to transaction participants, and global messaging where the state entity is visible to all the network participants. Both methods involve sharing the state entity in a distributed manner. The transaction model in private blockchains exposes the state data to all the participants in the network. However, in an ideal scenario, only specific stakeholders need to see certain data attributes - a pharmacy needs to see only the patient's prescription details and not the rest of the data for example. A GP may need access to the GP visits and diagnosis records but not hospitalization records. This is not the scenario with private blockchain frameworks by default as the EHR state entity is visible to all the participants within the healthcare network.

Private blockchain platforms implement various approaches that solve this problem and provide participant-specific data privacy mechanisms. These include *private data collections* [8] as part of Hyperledger Fabric as well other published methods such as the use of multi-party computation [9] or attribute-based encryption [10]. The following section explains in brief some of these existing methodologies as well as their limitations, followed by how our proposed approach using asymmetric encryption can be used for implementing granular privacy control in private blockchain networks.

2   Privacy in Private Blockchain Networks

In this section we describe existing approaches for implementing privacy in private blockchain networks, namely *private data collections* from Hyperledger Fabric, *multiparty communication* and *attribute based encryption* with a focus on their specific limitations.

2.1   Private Data Collections in Hyperledger Fabric

Hyperledger Fabric is a widely used private blockchain framework by the Linux Foundation and IBM. The distributed and decentralized model of Fabric makes the data visible across all the organizations. A group of organizations in the consortium might require some of the critical data to be shared amongst a subset of them, rather than sharing it across the entire network. Hyperledger Fabric provides the *private data collections* model to achieve this. A transaction with private data in Fabric is made up of two items, the actual private data and the hash of the private data as shown in Fig. 2. In this example, an EHR has a private data collection authorizing Org A/B/D. The private data is shared only with the organizations present in the collection whereas other organizations in the channel (Org C) are only able to see the hash of the private data.

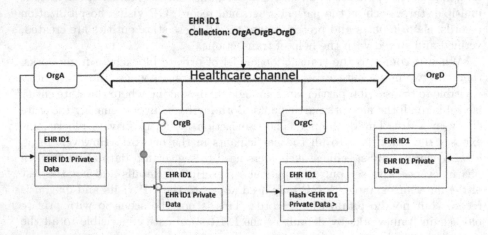

Fig. 2. A *private data collection* representation in a Hyperledger Fabric network

The problem with using private data collections is the potential number of private data collections which is exponentially proportional to the number of organizations in the network. For a modest network size of 6, there are 63 possible combinations, whereas increasing the organization count by one to 7, increases the combination size to 127. For 'n' number of organizations, the formula to calculate the possible private data collection combination is shown in Eq. 1, where R is recursive value of 1 till N.

$$\sum \frac{n!}{(n-R)! \times n!} \tag{1}$$

Another problem is that the private and public state data are stored in the world state ledger in a plain text format. A real world example of this is shown in Fig. 3 where the data highlighted in yellow clearly illustrates how private attributes can be easily recognized by explicitly accessing the world state ledger.

Fig. 3. Data persisted in the world state ledger in a Hyperledger Fabric network. The yellow highlighted aspects show attributes stored in plain text which are visible to all with access to the world state ledger. (Color figure online)

2.2 Multiparty Computation

Secure multi-party computation (MPC) [11] uses symmetric encryption for securing the private data owned by each organization in the network. This way the data is accessible only to the organizations with the required encryption key. All the organizations in the network must trust a secured MPC function executor module to execute the transactions containing private data. During the consensus phase, the private data is decrypted on-chain by the individual organizations and passed on to the MPC function module through gossip protocols. The module then returns the consensus, after processing the transaction with decrypted inputs from different organizations.

This method involves on-chain encryption and decryption of private data resulting in transaction overheads. Additionally a separate MPC function executor independent of the blockchain network needs to be established and maintained as well as a secure communication channel from each of the organizations in the network to the MPC module in order to share the private decrypted data in a secure manner.

2.3   Attribute Based Encryption

Attribute-based encryption [12] uses a cryptography key with reference to one or more attributes. A master secret key and a public key is initially generated with one or more attributes attached to it. The generated public key has n number of attributes attached to it. The private keys are then generated for each n number of attributes, using the master secret key and the individual attribute as input. Figure 4 illustrates how attribute-based encryption is used for privacy management in EHR use case.

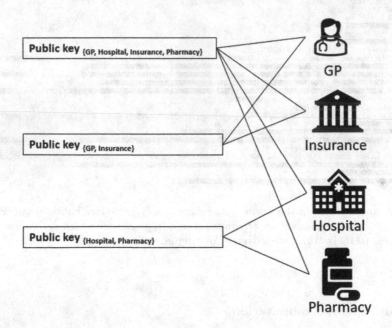

Fig. 4. Attribute based encryption for EHRs

The method has two limitations as discussed by the authors. The time complexity of the attribute-based encryption increases as the number of attributes increase as shown for both encryption and decryption in Eq. 2 and Eq. 3 for K attributes.

Encryption

$$[(2+n) \times K + 1] \times Cex + (2K+1) \times Cm + (2K+1) \times Cm \qquad (2)$$

Decryption

$$[(n+1) \times K + 1] \times Cp + n \times K \times Ce + [3 + (2+n) \times K] \times Cm \qquad (3)$$

For every possible set of attributes that are needed, a new public key has to be generated. If an attribute set has to be updated with an additional attribute, a new public key with the updated attribute set needs to be generated, followed by re-encrypting all the existing data with the newly generated public key.

3 Privacy Using Asymmetric Key Cryptography

The idea behind using asymmetric key cryptography for achieving privacy in private and permissioned blockchain networks is to assign an asymmetric key pair for each of the participants in the network. Each sensitive data field that needs to be secured (such as patient's hospitalization history or doctor visits in our example EHR use case) are encrypted using the public key(s) of the corresponding user(s) and persisted in the unique hash map. The encrypted data can only be then decrypted by the user with a corresponding private key. Any other user cannot decrypt the data unless the user with the correct key provides them with access.

For illustration purposes, we consider RSA [13] which is the most common form of asymmetric encryption. Some of the private blockchain frameworks depend on data consistency for consensus. Since blockchain networks execute the transactions on individual organizations as a sandbox, padding on encryption might produce a different encrypted output for different organizations. This may cause data inconsistency during the consensus phase. To avoid this, we can use the Electronic Code Book form of RSA encryption (RSA without padding) for private blockchain frameworks such as Hyperledger Fabric which depend on data consistency for its consensus.

3.1 Architecture

We use the following asymmetric cryptography specifications in our approach:

- Algorithm : RSA
- Cipher Mode : ECB (Electronic Code Book)
- Key Size : 256 bytes
- Padding : No Padding

On the state entity model, two different state models are used. One state exclusively handles the user's cryptographic key information and the other handles the actual data as shown in Fig. 5 for our example EHR use case.

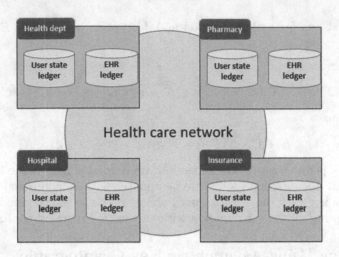

Fig. 5. Architecture of asymmetric cryptography for private blockchains for our example health care network use case

3.2 Workflow

In the following sections we describe the different steps of the workflow for user enrollment, data creation and adding and removing access using our Asymmetric Key Cryptography approach using our EHR use case.

User Enrollment. Each participating user in the network invokes this workflow once to retrieve their asymmetric key pair as illustrated in Fig. 6.

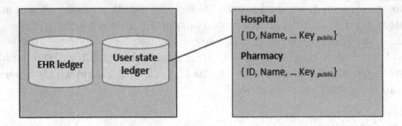

Fig. 6. User enrollment

EHR Creation. A normal invoke transaction is performed on the blockchain. The transaction may or may not process the private data. Public data like a patients general identity information are stored in plain text format, whereas private data such as hospitalization records are encrypted using the hospital's public key and persisted in a hash map as illustrated in Fig. 7.

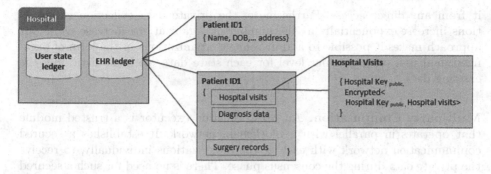

Fig. 7. Creating an electronic health record

Add Access. The user that has access to the private data attribute should invoke this transaction. If any other user apart from the hospital needs access to a patient hospitalization record, then the hospital user should invoke this workflow to provide them with access. To do so the hospitalization record in the decrypted format, along with the public key of the user requesting the access, is passed on to this workflow. A new entry is created in the hash map for the user requesting access as represented in Fig. 8.

The access can be removed later at anytime by the user by invoking the remove access workflow. The workflow removes the access for the specified user, by removing the entry against their public key from the hashmap.

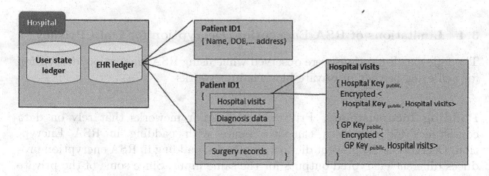

Fig. 8. Providing access to a new user

3.3   Comparison with the State of the Art

Hyperledger Fabric Private Data Collections. As demonstrated above, Hyperledger Fabric private data are stored as plain text in the world state ledger, whereas our approach stores the data in an encrypted format thus protecting it from any direct access. Furthermore, the private data collection combinations increase exponentially as the number of organizations increase while our approach makes it possible to add or remove organizations in the form of organizational user on a granular level for each state data, without disturbing the existing data.

Multiparty Computation. An MPC function executor is a trusted module that operates in parallel with a blockchain network. It establishes a secured communication network with each of the organizations individually, to receive the private data during the consensus phase. There is no need for such a secured channel network setup in our approach. Also, the data decryption performed on-chain increases the computation overhead, whereas our asymmetric cryptography approach handles the decryption of private data off-chain.

Attribute Based Encryption. Attribute-based encryption allows data to be encrypted for multiple attributes at once. It follows a one-to-many model, where data encrypted by a public key can be decrypted by the private key of each of the public key's attributes which is shown for EHRs previously in Fig. 4. The change in one attribute of an encrypted value can break the entire mapping and the whole encryption part needs to be performed again with a new set of attributes. On the other hand, using asymmetric cryptography we create a one-to-one model of private data. Any change in one attribute of the data does not affect other attributes, making it easy to add or remove the users at any point in time.

3.4   Limitations of RSA Encryption/Decryption for Data Privacy

The following limitations were observed while using RSA encryption/decryption for achieving privacy in private blockchain networks.

Padding Inconsistency. Private blockchain frameworks that rely on data consistency for consensus can face issues with padding in RSA Encryption/Decryption. To prevent dictionary attacks, padding in RSA encryption produces different encrypted outputs for the same input. Since some of the private blockchains such as Fabric depend on data consistency of executed transaction results during the consensus phase, using padding causes different transaction output from different organizations. This may cause the consensus to fail. To avoid this, padding is turned off for our approach, which makes it more prone to dictionary attacks.

Transaction Dependency on Encrypted Private Data. Transactions that are dependent on an encrypted private data attribute happen in two folds. First, the owner of the private data attribute queries the encrypted value from the blockchain and decrypts it off-chain. Second, the decrypted data is then forwarded to the dependent transaction. Frameworks like Hyperledger Fabric support transient maps to pass such sensitive data as part of a transaction. It ensures the data is available only during the execution phase and is flushed out after transaction completion.

Storage and Computation Overhead. The storage complexity of our approach increases linearly with an increase in the number of users since the encrypted entry for each authorized user is persisted separately in the hashmap. Any transaction creating a new version of the private state data has to recreate the hashmap with all the users present in it, which again increases the computation complexity linearly with an increase in the number of users. However, we believe that this linearly increasing storage and computation overhead is preferable to exponential increase experienced with other approaches.

4 Conclusion

We propose a novel approach of using RSA asymmetric key cryptography to enable data privacy on a fine-grain level for private and permissioned blockchain networks whereby each user can control the visibility of attribute(s) on a one-to-one basis. The decryption of encrypted data is handled at the authorized user end off-chain, which reduces the decryption processing overhead and improves the privacy factor for the private data. Whilst our approach also solves a number of other limitations with existing state-of-the-art methods, we have identified a number of challenges however these can be addressed in future work, such as utilising electronic code book (ECB) encryption with RSA for platforms with consensus models that are dependent on data consistency.

Acknowledgement. This work was supported by Enterprise Ireland and the Department of Enterprise, Trade and Employment through the Disruptive Technologies Innovation Fund (project number DT20180009).

References

1. Nakamoto, S.: Bitcoin: a peer-to-peer electronic cash system (2008). https://bitcoin.org/bitcoin.pdf
2. Ethereum. https://ethereum.org/en/
3. Hyperledger Fabric. https://www.hyperledger.org/use/fabric
4. R3 Corda. https://www.r3.com/corda-platform/
5. Guo, H., Li, W., Meamari, E., Shen, C.-C., Nejad, M.: The potential for blockchain to transform electronic health records. Harvard Bus. Rev. **3**, 2–5 (2017)
6. Guo, H., Li, W., Nejad, M., Shen, C.-C.: Access control for electronic health records with hybrid blockchain-edge architecture. In: 2019 IEEE International Conference on Blockchain, Atlanta, USA (2019)

7. Halamka, J.D., Ekblaw, A.: Attribute-based multi-signature and encryption for EHR management: a blockchain-based Solution. In: 2020 IEEE International Conference on Blockchain and Cryptocurrency (ICBC), pp. 1–5 (2020)
8. Hyperledger Fabric Private Data. https://hyperledger-fabric.readthedocs.io/en/release-2.2/private-data/private-data.html
9. Wang, X., Malozemoff, A.J., Katz, J.: EMP-toolkit: efficient multiparty computation toolkit (2016). https://github.com/emp-toolkit
10. Xu, H., He, Q., Li, X., Jiang, Bi., Qin, K.: BDSS-FA: A blockchain-based data security sharing platform with fine-grained access control. In: 2020 IEEE Access (ANTS), pp. 87552–87561 (2020)
11. Benhamouda, F., Halevi, S., Halevi, T.: Supporting private data on hyperledger fabric with secure multi party computation. IBM J. **63**(2/3), 3:1-3:8 (2019)
12. Rahulamathavan, Y., Phan, R.C.-W., Rajarajan, M., Misra, S., Kondoz, A.: Privacy-preserving blockchain based IoT ecosystem using attribute-based encryption. In: 2017 IEEE International Conference on Advanced Networks and Telecommunications Systems (ANTS), pp. 1–6 (2017)
13. Diffie, W., Hellman, M.: New directions in cryptography. IEEE Trans. Inf. Theory **22**, 644–654 (1976). https://doi.org/10.1109/TIT.1976.1055638

Short Paper Track

CBProf: Customisable Blockchain-as-a-Service Performance Profiler in Cloud Environments

Ruyue Xin, Jardenna Mohazzab, Zeshun Shi, and Zhiming Zhao[✉]

Multiscale Networked Systems (MNS) Research Group, University of Amsterdam,
Amsterdam, The Netherlands
{r.xin,z.shi2,z.zhao}@uva.nl

Abstract. Blockchain technologies, e.g., Hyperledger Fabric and Sawtooth, have been evolving rapidly during past years and enable potential decentralised innovations in a substantial amount of business applications, e.g. crowd journalism, car-sharing and energy trading. The development of decentralised business applications has to face challenges in selecting suitable blockchain technologies, customising network protocols among distributed peers, and optimising system performance to meet application requirements. Also, manually testing and comparing those different technologies are time-consuming. Therefore, an effective tool is needed for profiling the performance characteristics of blockchain services in different cloud environments. In this paper, we present the Customisable Blockchain-as-a-Service Performance Profiler (CBProf), a tool we developed for automating blockchain deployment and performance profiling in cloud environments. We also provide the implementation and functionality demonstration of this tool.

Keywords: Blockchain · Blockchain-as-a-Service (BaaS) · Automatic deployment · Performance profiling

1 Introduction

Blockchain technologies enable a secure, transparent, and decentralised environment to support transactions of data, goods, or financial resources [1]. Those technologies bring lots of opportunities for enterprises to enhancing their business processes in a decentralised manner. Permissioned blockchains are typical examples; they allow trusted and authorised entities to engage in blockchain activities to ensure privacy and security of enterprise information [13]. Cloud environments provide elastic and on-demand resources for customising data storage, processing, and communication, which play an increasingly important role for enterprises to operate blockchain-based decentralised applications (DApps) [12,15].

Permssioned blockchains like Hyperledger Fabric and Sawtooth have developed in recent years, and cloud resource is facilitated by an increasing number

© Springer Nature Switzerland AG 2022
K. Lee and L.-J. Zhang (Eds.): ICBC 2021, LNCS 12991, pp. 131–139, 2022.
https://doi.org/10.1007/978-3-030-96527-3_9

of providers, such as Amazon Web Services (AWS) and Microsoft Azure [4,5]. Therefore, developers need to ascertain the blockchain technologies and cloud provides best suited for their business purpose when transitioning from a classical application to a DApp [10]. To customise the configuration of a DApp in cloud environments, it is essential to determine the performance characteristics of different blockchains in different cloud situations, while profiling the performance of blockchains manual is rather time-consuming and undesirable [11]. Therefore, it becomes an urgent need to create a user-friendly tool to automatically deploy different configurations of blockchains on demand and provide insight into the performance by benchmarking the performance profiling results.

This paper presents a tool called Customisable Blockchain-as-a-Service Performance Profiler (CBProf), which implements automatic blockchain deployment on cloud environments and performance benchmarking and profiling for various blockchains. The rest of the paper is organised as follows: Sect. 2 analyses the requirements and describes related works. Section 3 presents CBProf architecture and function of each component. Section 4 is the implementation and demonstration of CBProf. Finally, Sect. 5 concludes this paper and provides a discussion about future work.

2   Requirements and Related Works

In this section, we analyse the requirements and challenges of a user-friendly blockchain performance profiler and provide related works based on requirements.

2.1   Requirements and Challenges

A user-friendly performance profiling tool is needed for developing and operating DApps in cloud environments. The tool should support a user to effectively customize the configuration of a blockchain network, automate the deployment of the blockchain services in cloud infrastructures, and explore the performance information collected from the runtime system. The tool has to consider the scenarios where the blockchain application has to run across different providers, e.g. for the reasons of improving fault tolerance, security and performance. However, the deployment of blockchain services across a distributed cloud environment involves provisioning of virtual machines (VMs), installing blockchain services, and customising the connectivity among blockchain nodes, which is not simple. Moreover, the performance of blockchains is influenced by many factors in the distributed cloud environment [7]; it is a challenge to build a precise performance model for a decentralized application.

2.2   Related Works

Based on the requirements of the user-friendly tool, we identify related works with automatic blockchain deployment and blockchain performance profiling.

Automatic Blockchain Deployment. Blockchain deployment on distributed environments is typically a time-consuming and cumbersome process, which leads to the research about automatic blockchain deployment. Frantz et al. propose a modelling approach that supports the semi-automated translation of human-readable contract representations into computational equivalents [2]. However, the automation in this research is only about smart contracts. Research by Shi et al. proposes a framework to automate the provision of required infrastructures and deploy Hyperledger Sawtooth [8]. We extend the research in this paper and provide a tool that supports more blockchain and is more user-friendly.

Automatic deployment tools such as Puppet[1] and Ansible[2] are commonly used but hard to integrate into invocation level automation, which is crucial for a user-friendly automatic deployment tool. However, CloudsStorm [14] which is developed for automatic deployment of cloud applications, can leverage different clouds and program them into cloud applications. Therefore, we develop our blockchain deployment tool integrating CloudsStorm. This tool is also integrated into our toolkit Software Defined Infrastructure Automator (SDIA)[3].

Blockchain Performance Profiling. For DApps, performance is a critical factor to consider according to application requirements. There already are many studies that focus on blockchain performance profiling. Pongnumkul et al. have contributed to performance analysis of Ethereum and Hyperledger Fabric with a varying number of transactions [6]. Shi et al. have studied the performance of one of Hyperledger Sawtooth in cloud environments [7]. The results provide insights for blockchain operators to optimise the performance of Sawtooth by adjusting configuration parameters. Currently, blockchain performance studies usually focus on several metrics or specific platforms [3,6,9]. Therefore, these studies cannot be used as a baseline when deploying a blockchain.

From related works, we can see that research into automation of blockchain deployment and performance profiling is very recent and usually separated into two topics. Therefore, an advanced framework is required to automate the complete process of blockchain deployment and performance profiling.

3   Customisable Blockchain-as-a-Service Performance Profiler

To meet the requirements in Sect. 2, we provide a performance profiler called CBProf in this section. We will introduce the functionality of each component in CBProf and how it works in detail.

---

[1] https://puppet.com/.
[2] https://www.ansible.com/.
[3] https://github.com/QCDIS/sdia-deployer.

3.1   Architecture and Functional Components

In CBProf (seen in Fig. 1), we design a blockchain deployment tool for automatic blockchain deployment and benchmarking and profiling tool for testing and profiling blockchain performance. Each tool contains several components.

Blockchain Deployment Tool. This tool processes blockchain deployment requests and facilitates deployment automatically. In Fig. 1, the **user input retriever** component collects blockchain deployment requests from users at first, such as VMs type, number and provider. After receiving blockchain configuration requirements, CloudsStorm, which is a framework for managing an application-defined infrastructure, is used for automatic deployment.

When deploying a blockchain in clouds, the nodes of a blockchain network are represented by VMs in clouds, and the nodes must form a network to ensure their communication with each other. Therefore, the blockchain deployment tool includes functions of VMs creation and communication. As for customised blockchain deployment, the blockchain deployment tool supports different blockchain platforms, such as Hyperledger Fabric and Sawtooth, and on different cloud provides, such as AWS and ExoGeni. All the blockchain services will be started automatically after deployment.

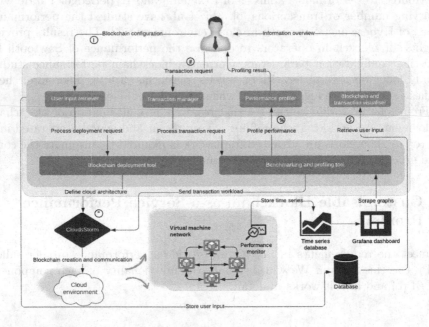

Fig. 1. Architecture of CBProf including blockchain deployment tool and benchmarking and profiling tool.

Benchmarking and Profiling Tool. The benchmarking tool processes and formats transaction requests so that it can simulate different business scenarios through which the functionality of the blockchain can be benchmarked. The profiling tool specifies the deployment of a performance monitor that records all blockchain processes, and it allows the monitor to collect the real-time performance data and stores it in a time-series database. Also, it can be used for profiling blockchain performance.

In Fig. 1, the **transaction manager** component allows for the specification, retrieval and storage of customised transaction requests, such as execution time and send rate of workloads can be ordered. Benchmark tools can be integrated into this component. After benchmarking, the **performance profiler** provides an overview and comparison of blockchain performance, such as the transaction latency and throughput (TPS). The comparison can provide users with a clear perspective regarding a specific purpose or a certain performance measure. As for **blockchain and transaction visualiser**, we design this component for collecting and visualising real-time blockchain performance data. The time-series database provides persistent storage on the local file system. And, a dashboard is configured to visualise data collected by the database. With this component, we can check many performance metrics like block number, committed transactions in real-time. This component is also interactive so that users can customise the performance of a specific period.

3.2   How CBProf Works

CBProf is a customisable automatic blockchain deployment and benchmarking tool. About customisation, CBProf provides choices with a) blockchain configuration including cloud provider, data centre, VMs number(blockchain nodes number), VMs type, blockchain platforms, and b) transaction request including execution time and send rate.

As shown in Fig. 1, CBProf works follow the process: 1) blockchain configuration is sent from users and stored in a database. 2) CloudsStorm will start the automatic deployment, including VMs launching, network configuration and VMs initialisation. Also, with CloudsStorm, blockchain initialisation on created VMs will be done at the same time. 3) After the blockchain is configured, transaction requests can be processes which is blockchain benchmarking with different patterns of transactions. 4) With a blockchain and transaction visualiser, users can check real-time blockchain performance. 5) Through a performance profiler, users can compare blockchain performance with different blockchain or transaction configurations. With CBProf, quick insight into the general performance of a blockchain can be acquired. Alternatively, when more in-depth and personalised analysis is desired, customised benchmark experiments can be configured by specifying benchmark artefacts.

4   Implementation and Demonstration

This section provides the implementation of CBProf and gives profiling results of blockchain performance comparing different configurations.

4.1   Implementation

We implement CBProf with many technologies. For the blockchain deployment tool, customised blockchain configuration is implemented by defining sub-topology, top-topology, infrastructure and execution code in CloudsStorm. Here, a script that accepts deployment configurations and automatically writes the code to create the blockchain configuration is also provided. In benchmarking and profiling tool, we integrate Hyperledger Caliper[4] for benchmarking the performance of blockchains. And, we deploy Prometheus[5] and Grafana[6] to collect and visualise real-time blockchain performance data. Besides, we use MongoDB[7] as the database to store user input information, and we build the GUI (graphical user interface) with Vue.js[8].

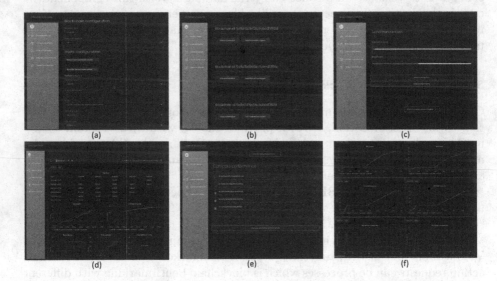

Fig. 2. CBProf tool interface and functions: (a) customise blockchain configuration; (b) overview of deployed blockchains; (c) transaction request; (d) performance visualization; (e) compare blockchain configuration; (f) compare blockchain performance

---

[4] https://github.com/hyperledger/caliper.
[5] https://prometheus.io/.
[6] https://grafana.com/.
[7] https://www.mongodb.com/.
[8] https://vuejs.org/.

4.2   Functionality Demonstrate

The tool interface can be seen in Fig. 2. The interface includes five functions: creating a blockchain, blockchain overview, comparing performance, comparing configuration and blockchain overview, which correspond to the architecture and components in Sect. 3.1. Users can use it to deploy different blockchains such as Hyperledger Fabric or Sawtooth on different cloud environments. Also, users can benchmark a blockchain with different transaction requests. Performance metrics can be seen in real-time during blockchain execution. And users can compare the performance of multiple blockchain configurations.

We also test the automatic deployment of Hyperledger Fabric on ExoGeni and AWS with CBProf. At first, for automatic blockchain deployment, we set up different fabric networks with 3, 6, 9, 12, 15 nodes and deploy them on ExoGeni and AWS clouds, respectively. All organisations of fabric network are a member of a single channel. VMs of ExoGeni are all XOSmall, and VMs of AWS are all t2.Small. Figure 3 shows the execution overhead of automatic deployment. It's obvious that ExoGeni consumes more time than AWS for any node number. Also, we can see that the consumption time of different nodes is similar, which means that the deployment is synchronised, and large-scale automatic blockchain deployment is possible with CBProf.

As for performance profiling, we provide a comparing of blockchain performance with different transaction requests. We do the benchmark for a three nodes fabric network. The transaction requests include both read and write operations. We set up send rates as 10, 20, 30, 40, 50 tps (transactions per second), and transaction duration as 100 s. Performance profile results can be seen in Fig. 4. Throughput is higher for query operation comparing with init operation, which is easy to understand because read operation needs fewer resources. And then, we can see that the throughout gradually stabilises when send rate is higher than 40. Therefore, send rate of 40 may be a bottleneck of this blockchain configuration. Performance profiling gives us an insight into blockchains capacity.

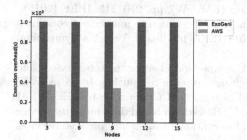

Fig. 3. Provision time of blockchain deployment

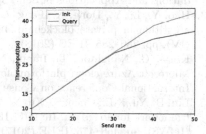

Fig. 4. Throughput of blockchain performance

5   Conclusion

In this paper, we provide the design and implementation of Customisable Blockchain-as-a-Service Performance Profiler (CBProf), a user-friendly tool that allows for convenient blockchain deployment and performance profiling. CBProf provides an approach to build a generic functionality that automatically defines the cloud architecture, the virtual machine network and the execution code to deploy the blockchain. Also, CBProf provides an approach to monitor the blockchain processes, visualise transaction execution processes and compare blockchain performance. Further in this paper, we present the implementation and functionality demonstration of CBProf. Moreover, we test the automation deployment for Hyperledger Fabric on cloud environments and provide the performance profiling results under different transaction requests. The results give us an overview of blockchain capacity under specific cloud environments.

The CBProf also collects many other monitor metrics such as resource usage and transaction flow data. In the future, we will develop more methods to detect anomalies for blockchain applications and provide adaptation strategies for meeting users requirements. Our tool allows for extension with open-source machine learning methods. We aim to make it an open framework and attract community effort to support more DApps related technologies.

Acknowledgment. This research is funded by the EU Horizon 2020 research and innovation program under grant agreements 825134 (ARTICONF project), 862409 (BlueCloud project) and 824068 (ENVRIFAIR project).

References

1. Abeyratne, S.A., Monfared, R.P.: Blockchain ready manufacturing supply chain using distributed ledger. Int. J. Res. Eng. Technol. **5**(9), 1–10 (2016)
2. Frantz, C.K., Nowostawski, M.: From institutions to code: towards automated generation of smart contracts. In: 2016 IEEE 1st International Workshops on Foundations and Applications of Self* Systems (FAS* W), pp. 210–215. IEEE (2016)
3. Hao, Y., Li, Y., Dong, X., Fang, L., Chen, P.: Performance analysis of consensus algorithm in private blockchain. In: 2018 IEEE Intelligent Vehicles Symposium (IV), pp. 280–285. IEEE (2018)
4. Kotas, C., Naughton, T., Imam, N.: A comparison of amazon web services and Microsoft Azure cloud platforms for high performance computing. In: 2018 IEEE International Conference on Consumer Electronics (ICCE), pp. 1–4. IEEE (2018)
5. Liu, B., Yu, X.L., Chen, S., Xu, X., Zhu, L.: Blockchain based data integrity service framework for IoT data. In: 2017 IEEE International Conference on Web Services (ICWS), pp. 468–475. IEEE (2017)
6. Pongnumkul, S., Siripanpornchana, C., Thajchayapong, S.: Performance analysis of private blockchain platforms in varying workloads. In: 2017 26th International Conference on Computer Communication and Networks (ICCCN), pp. 1–6. IEEE (2017)

7. Shi, Z., Zhou, H., Hu, Y., Jayachander, S., de Laat, C., Zhao, Z.: Operating permissioned blockchain in clouds: a performance study of hyperledger sawtooth. In: 2019 18th International Symposium on Parallel and Distributed Computing (ISPDC), pp. 50–57. IEEE (2019)
8. Shi, Z., Zhou, H., Surbiryala, J., Hu, Y., de Laat, C., Zhao, Z.: An automated customization and performance profiling framework for permissioned blockchains in a virtualized environment. In: 2019 IEEE International Conference on Cloud Computing Technology and Science (CloudCom), pp. 404–410. IEEE Computer Society (2019)
9. Sukhwani, H., Martínez, J.M., Chang, X., Trivedi, K.S., Rindos, A.: Performance modeling of PBFT consensus process for permissioned blockchain network (hyperledger fabric). In: 2017 IEEE 36th Symposium on Reliable Distributed Systems (SRDS), pp. 253–255. IEEE (2017)
10. Taş, R., Tanrıöver, Ö.Ö.: Building a decentralized application on the ethereum blockchain. In: 2019 3rd International Symposium on Multidisciplinary Studies and Innovative Technologies (ISMSIT), pp. 1–4. IEEE (2019)
11. Thakkar, P., Nathan, S., Viswanathan, B.: Performance benchmarking and optimizing hyperledger fabric blockchain platform. In: 2018 IEEE 26th International Symposium on Modeling, Analysis, and Simulation of Computer and Telecommunication Systems (MASCOTS), pp. 264–276. IEEE (2018)
12. Uriarte, R.B., Zhou, H., Kritikos, K., Shi, Z., Zhao, Z., De Nicola, R.: Distributed service-level agreement management with smart contracts and blockchain. Concurrency Comput. Pract. Exp. **33**, e5800 (2020)
13. Wüst, K., Gervais, A.: Do you need a blockchain? In: 2018 Crypto Valley Conference on Blockchain Technology (CVCBT), pp. 45–54. IEEE (2018)
14. Zhou, H., et al.: CloudsStorm: a framework for seamlessly programming and controlling virtual infrastructure functions during the DevOps lifecycle of cloud applications. Softw. Pract. Exp. **49**(10), 1421–1447 (2019)
15. Zhou, H., Ouyang, X., Ren, Z., Su, J., de Laat, C., Zhao, Z.: A blockchain based witness model for trustworthy cloud service level agreement enforcement. In: IEEE INFOCOM 2019-IEEE Conference on Computer Communications. IEEE (2019)

Author Index

Printed in the United States
by Baker & Taylor Publisher Services

Printed in the United States
by Baker & Taylor Publisher Services